A PLACE TO CALL HOME

After-School Programs For Urban Youth

Barton J. Hirsch

with contributions by
Nancy L. Deutsch

American Psychological Association
Washington, DC

Teachers College
Columbia University
New York and London

Published by
American Psychological Association
750 First Street, NE
Washington, DC 20002
www.apa.org

Teachers College Press
1234 Amsterdam Avenue
New York, NY 10027
www.tcpress.com

Typeset in Goudy by Page Grafx, Inc., St. Simons Island, GA

Printer: Data Reproductions, Auburn Hills, MI
Cover Designer: Go! Creative, Kensington, MD
Technical/Production Editor: Tiffany L. Klaff

Library of Congress Cataloging-in-Publication Data

Hirsch, Barton J.
    A place to call home: after-school programs for urban youth / Barton J. Hirsch.
        p. cm.
    Includes bibliographical references and index.
    ISBN 1-59147-202-4   ISBN 0-8077-4546-4 (softcover)
1. School-age child care—United States. 2. School-age child care—Activity programs—United States—Research 3. Poor children—United States—Social conditions. 4. Youth development—United States. I. Title.
    HQ778.63.H57 2005
    362.71'2—dc22
                                                                                2004018838

A *Place to Call Home* has been published under the following ISBNs:
APA: 1-59147-202-4
TCP: 0-8077-4546-4 (pbk.)

British Library Cataloguing-in-Publication Data
A CIP record is available from the British Library.

Printed in the United States of America
First Edition

To Margherita

CONTENTS

A PLACE TO
CALL HOME

PREFACE

This book examines six urban after-school centers, studied over a period of 4 years. Little has been written about the comprehensive after-school centers that are the subject of this book. Most academics have focused on a program or activity that corresponds to their scholarly interests. However, the need for good data and theory about comprehensive centers is pressing. Many in the policy world would like to see after-school programs focus exclusively on academics. Most of those who work in the after-school field beg to differ. Practitioners need more compelling data and theory to make their case. This book provides at least some of those scholarly supports.

Our years at these centers were full of excitement, mostly because the young people we spent time with, almost all of whom were African American or Hispanic early adolescents, had so much energy. Although their neighborhoods often overflowed with violence and their schools often felt like "jail," at these after-school sites they were able to enjoy being kids and connect with caring adult staff who provided wide-ranging mentoring. I hope to share some of that excitement and explain why I have come to believe that supporting these programs makes good sense.

At the same time, it is important for the after-school community to avoid complacency. Staff need to improve their mentoring skills, programs need to be more rigorous and challenging, and basic recreational opportunities need to be provided equitably to girls and boys. Accordingly, I offer a number of suggestions for improving after-school centers.

I did not begin this research as an advocate. In the beginning, I was neutral regarding the value of these settings. That is no longer true. Our cumulative set of data, both qualitative and quantitative, and the developmental theories that help to make sense of them have convinced me that the strengths and potential of these centers substantially outweigh their weaknesses and limitations.

My view of how to weigh the pros and cons reflects an appreciation of how difficult it is to create environments that match the needs of early adolescents. I have studied and taught for years about the failure of junior highs and middle schools to work well for this age group. And while conducting this research and writing this book, I have seen firsthand with my own children how poorly these schools do, even in a well-funded suburban school district. So when 74% of the youth we studied told us that these centers were a "second home" for them—a finding fully consonant with our own observations—it was not difficult to appreciate that, against the odds and despite their flaws, these settings had found a formula that worked. I hope to describe this formula.

This book is written for all of those who are concerned with afterschool programs, urban youth, or the social contexts of early adolescence—including the research community as well as those who are directly involved in the world of practice. Among researchers, the book will be of interest to both qualitative and quantitative researchers. The research involved a mixed method approach that used a variety of qualitative and quantitative procedures. Among those in the world of youth practice, the book will be useful to policymakers, administrators, and frontline youth workers.

These different groups tend to have contrasting preferences as to how a book of this sort should be written. I sympathize with the different orientations, as I have a background in practice as well as research and like to read both qualitative and quantitative reports.

I have enjoyed the challenge of writing this book in a way that each group will find accessible and agreeable. The qualitative findings are more fundamental to the theses of the book and so receive more attention than do the quantitative data. Detailed methodological and statistical points are placed in notes so that those who would like the details can have access to them. To keep the text as readable as possible, I have placed citations to prior publications as notes at the end of each chapter rather than putting them in the main body of the text.

The research began as a formative evaluation of an ambitious gender equity initiative at Boys & Girls Clubs and ultimately involved a very broad look at these centers. To provide maximum freedom to publish the research team's findings and views, whatever these might turn out to be, I negotiated an agreement with the clubs to keep their identity confidential. Accordingly, the location of the clubs is not specified and the names of all the sites have been changed, as have the names and certain identifying characteristics of individuals. I am extraordinarily grateful to the staff and youth at the clubs, and the executives at the regional headquarters, for their cooperation and support. Special thanks go to the director of the gender equity initiative. I also want to acknowledge the many helpful conversations I had with the consulting psychologist to the gender equity initiative. I regret that these individuals cannot be acknowledged by name because of the confidentiality agreement.

The research would have been much less interesting and ambitious without the collaboration of several gifted doctoral students. Many thanks to Nancy Deutsch, Tondra Loder, Maria Pagano, and Jennifer Roffman for their countless contributions. Nancy merits special recognition for co-authoring two of the chapters in this book. I also wish to thank Cathy Flynn for her help in launching the ethnographic component of the research. A variety of fellowships to these students provided additional funding for the research beyond that available from the Boys & Girls Clubs; we are grateful to the Northwestern University/University of Chicago Joint Center for Poverty Research, Spencer Foundation predoctoral research training grant to the School of Education and Social Policy at Northwestern University, Northwestern University Graduate School, and the Illinois Consortium for Educational Opportunity Program.

A large number of undergraduates, and a few master's students, did excellent field work at the clubs over the years. I gratefully acknowledge the contributions of Cecilia Bocanegra, Nithya Chandler, Nadia Cone, Lauren Eslicker, Amy Geary, Tyrone Gooch, Erin Higgins, Susan Israel, Diana Kalter, Miriam Landau, Jennifer Lind, Carrie Luo, Domonique McCord, Demetra Vranas, Sarah Watson, Terrenda White, and Kathryn Young.

I am indebted to a network of fine colleagues who generously commented on drafts of the book prospectus or individual chapters, or gave feedback on specific ideas. Thanks to Leslie Bloom, Lindsay Chase-Lansdale, John Diamond, Greg Duncan, Joseph Durlak, Jacquelynne Eccles, Denise Gottfredson, Robert Halpern, James Kelly, Carol Lee, Dan McAdams, Marjorie Orellana, Richard Price, Jean Rhodes, Stephanie Riger, Robert Schwartz, Edward Seidman, James Spillane, David Terman, and James Youniss. Special thanks go to David DuBois and Dan Lewis. My dean, Penelope Peterson, kindly granted me release time to work on the book and provided helpful suggestions on organizing the manuscript.

Thanks go as well to my editors at the American Psychological Association, Lansing Hays and Kristine Enderle. I am grateful to Carole Saltz at Teachers College Press for suggesting the possibility of copublishing the volume.

No simple thanks are adequate for my family: my wife, Margherita Andreotti, and my children, Rachel and David. They are truly a blessing.

A PLACE TO
CALL HOME

1

COMPETING DIRECTIONS FOR
AFTER-SCHOOL PROGRAMS

Across the political spectrum, there is enormous interest in how community-based organizations can help raise children growing up in poverty. Strengthening after-school programs has emerged as an important strategic approach at the federal, state, and local levels.[1] Guided activities and relationships with caring staff can lead to important developmental gains by increasing skills, instilling confidence, broadening cultural horizons, promoting positive values, and pointing youth in the right direction as they grow up.[2] Data from national polls indicate that after-school programs enjoy widespread public support.[3] In 2002, California voters overwhelmingly passed Proposition 49, providing increased funding for these programs.

Although after-school programs serve many young children, my focus—and that of this book—is on adolescents. Most children in that age group who are in after-school programs are early adolescents (ages 10–15). And it is for this group that the need for nurturing adults and institutions is most critical.

Early adolescence is a time of great developmental change. The body changes in all kinds of mysterious, and often embarrassing, ways. The transition from the small, personal elementary school to the larger and more impersonal environment of the middle school or junior high heralds a less welcoming academic atmosphere and upheavals in peer friendship groups.

The opportunities for engaging in risky behaviors (e.g., drugs, sex) increase substantially, as do the possibilities for gang involvement. Just at the time when parental guidance can be most helpful, that relationship is strained as well. Adolescents and their parents frequently experience less closeness and more conflict around the time of puberty, as the end of childhood and the beginning of adolescence beckon.[4]

Children need adults they can rely on and trust to help them adjust to these diverse changes. Teachers could fill this need but they do not. Throughout the 20th century, and continuing to this day, educators have sought to design schools suited to the distinct needs of early adolescents, but their efforts, first with junior highs and later with middle schools, are generally acknowledged to have missed the mark.[5] Students' reported satisfaction with the quality of school life plunges.[6] The school's departmentalized structure often results in teachers more committed to their academic subjects than to their students—and with 100 or more students each day, how well could teachers get to know students even if they tried? So, teachers, too, are not able, and sometimes not even willing, to fill the needs of early adolescents for significant relationships with wise and caring adults. As William Damon lamented, "[Y]oung people everywhere today are lacking guidance. They listen fruitlessly for voices that do not speak."[7] After-school programs can be an important site for the mentoring that young people from poor neighborhoods need.

Adolescents need places where they learn and have fun, but many low-income, urban neighborhoods are dangerous places. Gang violence is rampant. Many youth shy away from city parks, wary of being assaulted or confronted by drug dealers. Malls—popular places to hang out among suburban youth—do not exist in or near these neighborhoods. Even their apartments can feel unsafe, with the sound of gunshots nearby. After-school centers can provide the safety and relief from violence that are so desperately needed.

In addition to direct benefits to young people themselves, after-school programs can support the people who are most crucial to youth: their parents.[8] Whether married or single, parents in low-income communities need to work. In today's economy, low-wage jobs are increasingly available only during late afternoon, evening, and weekend hours.[9] Yet these are precisely the times when youth are not in school. These types of jobs offer little flexibility to parents to check on their children and monitor their behavior. This is particularly unfortunate given that so many low-income families live in neighborhoods that present real dangers to children. Moreover, being on the job makes it very difficult to help children with their homework, although increasing parental involvement is an important goal of many school reform efforts. After-school programs address these needs, providing the supervision and homework assistance that parents cannot provide while on the job.

Recent welfare reforms have resulted in more mothers entering the workforce from low-income communities. The effect this has on adolescent offspring is unclear. Some studies reveal an increase in problem behavior, whereas others find no change or even benefits.[10] To the extent that welfare policy results in harm to adolescents, the importance of the support that after-school programs provide to working parents—and their communities—will only increase.

Community-based youth programs may also support school reform efforts. The failures of urban schools are many, deep, and widely known. Widespread efforts at reform have generated isolated success stories, but it is unclear whether gains at particular schools or districts can be sustained and increased, and whether any of these individual successes provide a viable model for national dissemination. A recent meta-analysis of evaluation research, which uses statistical techniques to synthesize results across studies, indicates that the level of success, even for the best known reforms, is modest.[11] It is clear that schools need all the help that they can get. After-school programs are seen as providing important supports to school-based efforts. After-school programs can provide tutors and mentors who can promote skill development and reinforce high academic expectations. Among possible ways to enhance learning beyond the regular school day, after-school programs appear to be a natural venue for efforts to enhance school reform efforts.

Into this void of adult leaders, into this gap in the parental, educational, and community support systems, steps the after-school program. Or so everyone hopes. After-school programs have been around for a long time and clearly have relevant strengths. Yet there is no clear consensus about overarching goals and program design. Many of these controversies are not new and it is worth gaining some historical perspective.

AFTER-SCHOOL PROGRAMS: PAST, PRESENT, AND FUTURE

After-school programs first emerged on the American scene in the latter part of the 19th century.[12] Storefronts, settlement houses, and churches began to offer spaces away from the city streets for young people to congregate safely, have fun, learn useful skills, and be exposed to the socializing influence of adults. As local sites proliferated, they began to organize themselves into national organizations of Boys Clubs, Ys, Scouts, 4-H, Junior Achievement, and so on. Today, the 40 largest national youth organizations serve approximately 40 million youth.[13]

Not all youth were equally served by these programs. Most sites were oriented toward boys rather than girls. Separate girls-only programs were developed, but they were never as plentiful as those for boys. Several of these gender-specific national organizations came together toward the end of the 20th century, with the merger of Big Brothers and Big Sisters in 1977 and the formation of a coed Boys & Girls Clubs of America in 1990. African Americans, too, had fewer sites and funding for after-school activities, a trend that continues to the present day. In the 1920s, only 2 out of 225 new playgrounds in New York City were built in Black neighborhoods.[14] There continues to be a paucity of after-school programs that serve low-income urban communities as compared with those in affluent suburbs.[15]

There has been a certain stability in the activities offered by programs. As Robert Halpern noted in the following:

> The basic activity structure that emerged early on among after-school programs changed little over the decades, with clubs and classes, arts and crafts and table games, indoor or outdoor physical activity, cultural activity, and occasional field trips. Participation in the visual and expressive arts has been a constant. Specific emphases have risen or fallen. Pre-vocational activities such as metal-work declined over time. Yesterday's radio clubs have been replaced by today's computer clubs. Academic concerns emerged in the 1960s, and since then most programs have included homework time, perhaps some tutoring, and reading time.[16]

Of course, program content has not been without controversy. Several of the main tensions that exist today, and have existed for some time, grow out of the broader rationales that have been offered for youth programs. What is the relationship of after-school programs to schools? To what extent should after-school programs focus on preventing problem behavior versus promoting normal development?

There has been increased interest over the past few decades in having after-school programs support academic achievement. It is hard to disagree with this goal in the abstract. Yet does this mean that academic support should be the primary mission of after-school programs? And how should academic programs be designed for after-school settings?

Although some after-school programs are primarily academically oriented, many see their mission more broadly, as fostering growth in a wide range of skills and domains. Academics is important, but other areas are important as well. If providing academic assistance were to become the core mission, that would involve significant reductions in other activity areas. It also would likely require substantial new training, which would be a recurring cost given high staff turnover rates.

Even if there could be agreement about the place of academically oriented activities in after-school programs, how programs go about providing that support is not at all clear. Some advocates see after-school programs as sites for additional time for drilling in core academic competencies. Those who provide curricula to schools see after-school programs as additional markets for standardized material. In short, many of those in schools, or used to working with schools, see after-school as a natural extension of what happens in school. The perspective of those who work in the after-school arena is often dramatically different. As one coordinator of after-school literacy programs asked skeptically, "Why would you want to extend the goals and methods of a failed system into the after-school hours?"[17] Such an attitude is not new. For most of the past century, after-school was perceived in part as an antidote to school. School was seen as a place where low-income and minority youth were treated with condescension, where strengths were neither understood nor appreciated. When youth got out of school and came to community youth sites, many program staff felt that they had to undo the damage that school had done to youth. After-school programs also have believed that they should experiment with alternative, more creative ways of helping students learn.

There are similar tensions regarding prevention programs. Over the past 2 decades, a number of highly structured programs have been developed to prevent the onset of an array of problem behaviors—drug use, delinquency, teen sex, and so on. Although most such programs were implemented in school, after-school sites are seen as attractive sites for dissemination. A concern with youth problem behaviors has always been part of the justification for after-school programming, but most sites over the years have resisted making it the dominant focus. However, the new demand for accountability increases the pressure to use preventive programs that have a history of documented success—though that efficacy has usually been demonstrated in school, rather than in voluntary after-school settings where youth do not have to participate in the program or come to the site in the first place. Just as with academics, questions arise as to how much emphasis to put on problem prevention versus promoting normal development, and how implementing highly structured programs fits with the more informal setting of most after-school programs.

WHAT RESEARCH DOES— AND DOES NOT—TELL US

The National Research Council (NRC) and Institute of Medicine (IOM) published a major review of community youth programs in 2002. In examining program effectiveness, the NRC/IOM report relied heavily on results from existing literature reviews. Particular emphasis was placed on the most methodologically rigorous, experimental evaluations of program effects. The NRC/IOM report identified a number of programs that have produced positive developmental gains and reduced indices of problem behavior and psychological dysfunction. This is a welcome finding. Furthermore, the overall excellence of the report, particularly in the guidelines it provides for future research, helps to advance the field. Nevertheless, there are important limitations to the report—and the state of the field. Two sets of limitations are of special importance to the work reported in this book.

First, the number of well-designed evaluation studies is not great. The number of such studies, moreover, would shrink dramatically were it not for the NRC/IOM's highly elastic definition of community programs. For example, programs that are implemented by schools during the regular school day are counted as community programs. Under this expansive notion of community, it is hard to know what would not be considered a community program.[18] This is not hairsplitting, as the overwhelming number of studies reviewed in these meta-analyses are school-based. In the meta-analyses of Joseph Durlak and Anne Wells, for example, which are prominently cited in the NRC/IOM report, school-based programs account for 73% of primary prevention programs reviewed and for 93% of secondary prevention programs.[19]

In addition to being school-based, a number of other features of the evaluation studies that are cited call into question their applicability to community-based settings. The use of highly specified intervention manuals is one such characteristic. These manuals have a legitimate purpose in seeking to increase the likelihood that an intervention will be delivered as designed. In the report by the Social Development Research Group at the University of Washington, which also is prominently cited by the NRC/IOM, 96% of the evaluation studies reviewed used a manual or other form of structured curricula.[20] However, most community programs do not use manuals or highly structured programs; when they do, they are unlikely to follow the prescriptions in the lockstep, detailed way that is presumed by the curricular developers (and, often, evaluators).

Most evaluation studies, indeed, do not address how well the intervention is actually implemented. The NRC/IOM report acknowledges this limitation but does not discuss it. To do so might have led them to question the generalizability of the studies that they reviewed. Consider this for a moment. Most of the research reviewed represents demonstration projects that receive high levels of project support. Even here, however, the implementation analyses that have been conducted often reveal a significant gap between the program that is supposed to be delivered and what actually occurs on the ground.[21] It is quite likely that the fidelity of the program as delivered will be even weaker under ordinary program conditions, when staff do not have access to, and are not concerned about, feedback from research staff and consultants. Thus, existing studies do not provide much information about the *effectiveness* of programs under normal operating conditions, as opposed to what the NRC/IOM refers to as their *efficacy* under highly supported conditions.[22]

The information yield from existing evaluation studies is limited as well by another factor that the NRC/IOM does emphasize: Even when studies demonstrate a positive outcome, the research is not designed in a manner that helps us to understand why gains came about. A theory of change is rarely specified in sufficient detail, and the processes that may underlie positive change are not measured. Nor are a sufficient number of comparison groups used that might allow researchers to tease out causal from noncausal factors. So there is little understanding about why interventions work or do not work.

Similar problems arise when turning from studies that have examined psychosocial programs, such as the NRC/IOM report, to those that have evaluated academically focused programs, which were recently reviewed by Fashola.[23] The overwhelming number of studies dealt with younger children. Although several programs had been extended to after-school hours, almost all of the evaluation data were from interventions delivered in school during regular school hours. Implementation issues and processes that underlie change receive scant attention.

A good deal of what is currently known about after-school programs comes from studies that focus on process rather than outcome. The best known of these is by Milbrey McLaughlin and colleagues.[24] This work examined exemplary youth development programs across the country, focusing on programs for adolescents. The research included repeated observations and interviews. McLaughlin and associates found that there was no single prototype for the successful program. Rather, the content of successful programs drew on the unique interests of individual staff. Caring staff who were highly motivated to work with youth, and who were responsive to youth interests and input, was the key.

Robert Halpern and associates examined what they considered to be typical or garden-variety after-school programs.[25] They, too, found that caring staff and attentiveness to youth empowerment characterized the better programs. Youth were drawn to less structured activities and did not favor structured programs. Thus, in true community sites where youth could vote "with their feet" whether or not to participate, there was little interest among young people, and sometimes even outright hostility, to the kind of highly scripted curricula that was the focus of NRC/IOM attention. By focusing on typical rather than exemplary programs, Halpern and associates discovered that program quality varied considerably. At some sites, staff were uninvolved, unenthused, or ill prepared to address youth needs. Such poorly run programs did keep youth safe and off the streets—not a trivial concern in violent neighborhoods—but appeared to do little to promote positive development.

Quite a few program evaluations also document youth activities. These often provide useful information and I draw on this information throughout the book. However, the quality of the research varies considerably.[26] Among quantitative studies, many are not subject to more than rudimentary statistical analysis. Qualitative research is often limited in the depth of assessment. For example, although the research can include observations by outside research staff, the logistics frequently demand that schedules be set up considerably beforehand, alerting program staff to impending site visits. This foreknowledge can easily affect staff performance, so that the researchers may be observing peak performance, rather than typical operation, which results in judgments about program quality that are inflated to an unknown degree. Thus, considerable caution must be exercised about such reports. In contrast, the studies by the McLaughlin and Halpern teams involved repeated observations.

If by now you were to surmise that the research that has actually been done on after-school programs is quite limited, you would be right. That is not to say that little has been written on this field. An ever-growing number of edited books, journal issues, and paper collections on Web sites discuss these programs. The offerings are mostly alternative conceptualizations, strategic marketing plans, and so on. What is rarely found are papers that present original empirical data. This state of the field is not unusual for a new and emerging area of research. So we should not be overly critical. Yet neither should we be complacent. A lot more data, linked to theory and practice, is needed.

CENTRAL CONCERNS OF THIS BOOK

The research reported in this book was conducted over a 4-year period at six urban after-school sites affiliated with the Boys & Girls Clubs of America. These clubs are comprehensive youth development sites, offering activities in many areas including recreation, academic support, psychoeducational programs, arts, computers, field trips for cultural enrichment, entrepreneurship (including fund-raising), dances, movies, and so on. The clubs were more of the garden-variety than exemplary type, though one of the clubs was considered the crown jewel of those in the area. These types of youth settings have not been the subject of much theorizing or published empirical research.[27] University researchers have been drawn to the design and study of highly structured programs that reflect their specific scholarly interests rather than comprehensive settings, which are much less structured. Programs designed by university researchers tend to focus on specific academic or psychosocial skills; comprehensive sites seek to promote development across a wide range of domains, help youth deal with the many stressors of growing up in low-income neighborhoods, and guide them toward developing attitudes and behaviors that will be of general use in preparing for adult life. Because these comprehensive settings have drawn little attention from researchers, the rationale for their designs has received less theoretical articulation. To develop that theoretical rationale, I devote considerable attention to what we (my research assistants and I) found the clubs do best. These are their core strengths, the foundational elements on which they can build.

Although the research is based on Boys & Girls Clubs, the findings are not limited to this specific organization. Having reviewed the literature on programs at varied sites, observed other sites, and talked with investigators who have studied other programs, I believe that the results are applicable to many comprehensive urban after-school programs for this age group. For example, there is considerable overlap between activities offered in these clubs and those provided at the NYC Beacons.[28] The Beacons are located in public schools, with the after-school program run by community-based organizations. Programs include recreational, social service, educational enrichment, and vocational activities.

At the same time, there is a fundamental difference between these clubs and some after-school sites in the strength of mentoring relationships between program staff and youth. Mentoring is one of the core strengths of the clubs we studied and is a strong component of the NYC Beacons and many other programs. However, findings from the recent, initial evaluation of the 21st Century Community Learning Centers suggest that staff mentoring is much weaker at those sites. The 21st Century Centers are located in public schools in more than 1,400 school districts and communities nationwide. Teachers, the primary staff at the federally funded 21st Century Centers, often had limited enthusiasm for working in the after-school program, and the amount of time spent at the site by staff and youth was modest.[29] Although the evaluation does not directly address the strength of youth–staff ties at the Centers, it is difficult to imagine that they were very powerful under those circumstances. These factors may help to explain the negligible impact the Centers had on youth academic and psychosocial outcomes. Thus, it is especially timely to understand the ways in which strong mentoring can benefit youth in urban after-school programs, which is an overarching objective of this book.

I began this research sympathetic to structured programs and I remain intrigued by their potential, but my enthusiasm has been tempered by real-world difficulties in implementing these programs as designed. In addition, my view of how such programs work in garden-variety sites has shifted and I now place much greater emphasis on how such programs foster effective relationships between youth and staff. As the research team spent time in the clubs, our attention was repeatedly drawn to the benefits for youth of less structured programs. In particular, we could not fail to notice the exceptional quality of youth–staff relationships, a quality that also was reflected in our quantitative analyses of the linkage between these relationships and youth well-being. We came to appreciate that these settings have exceptional power. Thus, I did not enter the clubs with a positive bias or as an advocate; rather, findings from our empirical research, and especially the convergence of qualitative and quantitative results, persuaded me of their worth.

Furthermore, this book is far from a blanket endorsement of these sites as I do not shy away from discussing problems and limitations.

The principal aim of the book is to provide theoretically embedded data that highlight the value and potential of comprehensive urban after-school programs with strong youth–staff relationships. The potential is considered through an examination of both strengths and weaknesses. The theoretical rationale for this type of after-school program focuses on two central elements.

The first foundational element is recreation. Basketball, volleyball, table tennis, and the like are typically disparaged as program elements among university researchers as well as policymakers. However, children love to have fun with their friends and are drawn to after-school programs because the recreational activities allow them to do just that. And where else can they do so with safety in neighborhoods where city parks are often places for drug dealing and violence? Savvy staff communicate their appreciation of youth culture, using it as a vehicle to respect youth strengths and interests, avoiding a deficit orientation (i.e., focus on their problems) that turns youth off. Having thus established themselves as "cool," staff now have the credibility to mentor youth more effectively.

Mentoring of youth by after-school staff is the greatest strength and core foundation of these programs. Staff mentor youth around varied life concerns, from understanding pubertal changes, to avoiding violent confrontations, to becoming comfortable interacting with well-to-do White adults. They provide knowledge, encourage positive attitudes, and teach the skills and discipline needed for success in life. Yes, they help with homework—indeed, more so than do teachers or kin—but their top priority is the broader educational task of preparing youngsters to grow up and take their place as productive members of society.

Programs are also important, but not in the way envisioned by those who create structured curricula. Strict adherence to curricula tasks is not something done well at these sites, though they are rarely done well even in schools that have experience with structured programs. Given the inconsistent quality of implementation, formal programs are not a core strength or foundation of these after-school organizations. However, programs are valuable in providing contexts that encourage staff to extend their mentoring beyond their normal limits.

Within our focus on recreation, relationships, and programs, we pay special attention to gender. For most of the 20th century, these clubs were Boys Clubs, and it was less than 2 decades ago that they became coed Boys & Girls Clubs. The executive leadership at this regional affiliate of the Boys & Girls Clubs of America had concluded that girls were being underserved by the clubs. They then launched a gender equity initiative that focused on strengthening programs for girls. Our research involvement began when they asked me to evaluate this effort. Because we believed that we could not adequately understand the experience of girls without studying the experience of boys, we studied both.

Although much of our effort was devoted to the evaluation of the gender equity initiative, we took a very broad look at club operations because the impact of this initiative was designed to be widespread. In addition, part of the funding for the evaluation required that it contribute to the expansion of the research base on girls' development in minority communities. So we took on a large mandate, evaluating and giving ongoing feedback, yet also addressing underlying processes in depth with the emergent goal of helping to elaborate a vision for what the clubs could accomplish.

Drawing on these multiple interests, I aim in this book to contribute to theory and practice. Each chapter draws on literatures across disciplines to provide the basis for an integrative analysis. The chapter on the club as a second home, for example, synthesizes literature from fields ranging from environmental psychology to landscape architecture; the chapter on program implementation attends to the overlap in the literatures in political science, education, and clinical and community psychology; and the chapter on mentoring considers meta-analysis of formal mentoring programs, conceptualizations of the self in relationships ranging from Harter and the classical symbolic interactionists to Kohut and clinical psychoanalysis, and sociocultural studies of codeswitching. Theory development is closely linked to empirical data. The research emphasized the use of multiple methods, something quite unusual for this new field. Participant observation, survey questionnaires, and structured as well as unstructured interviews all generated important data.

It is hoped that this wide-ranging empirical and theoretical inquiry will clarify the value of comprehensive urban after-school programs of the sort that were studied. The range of theory and methods used should help spark new interest in these programs and organizations among a wide range of scholars.[30] As the philosopher of science Abraham Kaplan declared, "The dangers are not in working with models but in working with too few, and those too much alike, and above all, in belittling any effort to work with anything else."[31]

OUR STRATEGIES FOR GETTING TO KNOW
THE CLUBS AND YOUTH

At this point I would like to discuss briefly the kinds of data we collected, some of the methodological issues that we faced, and the rationale for the choices that were made.

Most of the time we spent in the six after-school centers was as ethnographers. We were classic participants–observers. We played volleyball, basketball, and table tennis; helped put up bulletin boards; and sat in on psychoeducational programs. We also had ongoing informal conversations with youth and staff about goings-on both in and outside of the club, and carefully observed patterns of activity and interaction. Occasionally, when one of the researchers was the only adult in the room and things had gotten out of hand, we helped to restore order. I do not think that such limited interventions detracted from the relationships we established at the site; indeed, I think that to do otherwise would have seemed odd to both youth and staff.[32]

We sought to have a team of observers at most sites for a number of reasons: The clubs were fast-paced environments and important interactions might be missed with only a single observer, it enabled us to increase the number of observational days per week per site, and it allowed us to provide training opportunities to graduate and undergraduate students interested in youth development.

A full team consisted of a doctoral student and two undergraduates. At the beginning of their placement (in the fall), the team went on the same day, which allowed for coverage of varied activities and for better training and supervision. As the academic year progressed and we started to gain an understanding of the site, to increase our coverage the doctoral student often went on separate days from the undergraduates, and beginning in the winter, the two undergraduates sometimes went on different days as well. Accordingly, we were in each club from 1 to 3 days a week, typically from early October through early June. A partial team consisted of a doctoral student and one master's-level student or two undergraduates. As with any research project, our resources were limited, and in Year 2 of the research, we were able to make only 2- to 3-day follow-up site visits to the centers we had studied with full teams during Year 1. A complete listing of coverage per site over the 4 years of this study is provided in Table 1.1.

Each ethnographer recorded detailed field notes after leaving the center. These were discussed at weekly research meetings during which we compared observations across observers at each club, across clubs, and eventually

TABLE 1.1
Observational Assessment by Club

	Year 1	Year 2	Year 3	Year 4
West River	Full	Site visit		
New City	Full	Site visit		
Midwest	Full	Site visit		
Clemente	Full	Site visit	Partial[a]	
East Side		Full	Full	Partial[b]
North River		Full		

Note. Full = One doctoral student + two undergraduate students.
[a]Two undergraduate students. [b]One doctoral student + one master's-level student.

across years. These constant comparisons helped us sharpen our observations and understanding and focus our plans for additional data collection. Some of these observations led directly to more focused research investigations (e.g., our observation of Sammy writing his application for Youth of the Year, detailed at the beginning of chap. 3, was a major impetus toward launching our study of the after-school center as a second home).

In addition, I spent some observational time at the clubs and interviewed all of the club directors. I also interviewed a number of executives at the regional headquarters and participated in several meetings there.

In a few instances, I quote extensively from the field notes regarding important substantive issues. Readers need access to the original data so that they can more effectively critique our interpretation. If this field is going to advance, we need some commonly available qualitative data to which everyone can refer.

With one exception, all of the student ethnographers were female. Approximately 40% of these observers were individuals of color, and they were distributed over five of the clubs. All of the students brought distinctive life experiences and competencies to the project. The minority student researchers had distinctive strengths, as did the others. The African American student researchers, for example, as a rule tended to develop relationships more quickly at the African American centers and to have a greater wealth of experiences and theoretical background in issues relating to African American culture. At the same time, the nonminority researchers also had strong interpersonal and organizational skills and were able to develop good rapport at all of the sites; they also contributed their own distinctive theoretical and methodological areas of expertise. This diversity, in my view, enhanced the project considerably.

Our observations were also compared with observations that were made by the director of the gender equity initiative, who made frequent visits to all of the clubs (including ones not included in our study). In addition, a psychologist who had been hired to conduct gender equity workshops at each club made her own observations. I talked frequently with the director of the gender equity initiative and the consulting psychologist; these conversations provided an unusually wide breadth and depth of observational data.

A final check on all of the data we obtained (including the questionnaire and interview data) was provided when we presented our findings, first orally and then in writing, to each of the clubs and to various groups at the regional headquarters. In some instances, we needed to revise our data or understanding, but in general the feedback validated our findings. An initial draft of this book was also provided to the regional headquarters.

The fact that we were conducting a formative evaluation that was intended to provide feedback on the gender equity initiative influenced the weight we put on ethnographic data. The clubs are distinct environments, and we needed to understand them inside and out for us to have credibility when we presented our reports. I have worked as a practitioner, and I know that I would be quite skeptical of any presumed expert who did not have a concrete understanding of my work. In addition, given that we had to produce a report each year approximately 6 months after starting that year's data collection, relying primarily on sophisticated statistical analyses of quantitative data was simply not feasible.

We did not want to depend entirely on observational data because each method has its own limitations. So we also conducted a large survey as well as structured and unstructured interviews. Our involvement in the club as ethnographers helped us develop close relationships which, I believe, enabled us to obtain better quality survey and interview data.

The survey was administered to youth ages 10 to 18 during our first year, at the four clubs that were studied that year. The survey was conducted during the winter, when attendance was highest. We came to each club for 4 days over the same 2-week period. By the fourth day, new respondents were minimal. Of the 306 eligible children approached, a total of 300 (98%) agreed to participate. Several research staff (including a Spanish-speaking Latina researcher for the Hispanic clubs) were on hand to help any youth who had difficulty reading any of the items. This sample had a median age of 13.38 years (SD [standard deviation] = 2.76) and was 59% male, 68% African American and 32% Hispanic, with 79% receiving free or reduced-price lunch at school.

Important data were also collected during a structured interview conducted during Year 1 at those four clubs. I refer to this as our main interview sample. The participation rate was again about 98%. The 112 youth in this interview were split evenly by club and gender, had a mean age of 12.92 years (range = 10–18; SD = 2.39), and were 59% African American and 41% Hispanic, with 86% receiving free or reduced-price school lunch. A total of 25% of the mothers of the interviewed children did not complete high school, 45% had received a high school diploma, and 30% had some college. Sixty percent of these youth lived in single-parent households.

Youth in both the survey and main interview samples participated quite actively in the club. An overwhelming majority of survey sample youth (84%) came to the club at least 3 days a week, with half (51%) coming all 5 days. Nearly 70% stayed at the club 2 to 4 hours each visit. The numbers are comparable for the main interview sample, with 88% coming at least 3 days a week (55% came 5 days a week) and 80% staying 2 to 4 hours per visit. Similar high attendance rates were reported for the NYC Beacons.[33] These figures contrast markedly with participation rates at the 21st Century Community Learning Centers and at the San Francisco Beacons, where middle school students attended on average only 1 day per week, and at the Extended-Service Schools, where average attendance for this age group was less than twice per week.[34] It should be clear, therefore, that our sites represent high-attendance settings, the kind of participation that is most likely to have a significant impact on youth. At the same time, readers are cautioned that some of the findings we report may not be characteristic of low-attendance settings.

The main interview was conducted during the late winter and spring, after the researchers had been at each club for several months and had developed good rapport. The interviewers read each question aloud to the interviewee. This interview was the source of important qualitative data (e.g., regarding the club as a second home) and also generated important quantitative data. These data were part of the overall research cycle; just as our observations led us to assess certain domains in the survey and interview, some of the latter findings led to areas of focused ethnographic research. Each young person was given a $10 gift certificate for participating in the interview.

The low-income nature of the sample reflects the communities in which the after-school programs are located. All of the centers were in the poorest one third of neighborhoods in the city. Two were part of public housing projects. All but one ranked in the top one half of community areas in terms of rates of violent crimes. There tended to be three gangs in the general vicinity of each site.

Because we wanted to use our personnel efficiently and gather sufficient data for quantitative analyses, we studied only the larger clubs in the area. A majority of the larger clubs participated in the research; from what we know of the other large clubs that did not participate, the participating clubs are not a biased sample of those that drew predominantly minority youth.

OUTLINE OF THE BOOK

Part I of the book discusses relationships in the clubs, which is what the clubs do best. Chapter 2 discusses how peer ties affect program recruitment, retention, and implementation. Most fundamentally, they allow these young people to just be kids, in neighborhoods where this is otherwise impossible. Arguments are detailed for why policymakers should fund recreation programs. Chapter 3 considers how these comprehensive settings can serve as a second home for urban youth. The respective contributions of relationships and the physical setting are considered in terms of making the space into a place in which youth feel at home. Chapter 4 focuses on mentoring. There is an extensive discussion of how one adult male staff person draws on folk ways of mentoring to provide guidance for the young men at his club. These data are interpreted within a theoretical model that emphasizes the importance of identity development during adolescence. The chapter then turns to a quantitative analysis of the linkage between youth–staff relationships and measures of youth well-being. The value of youth–staff relationships is compared with that of youth–kin and youth–teacher ties.

Part II turns to a more extensive discussion of some of the weaknesses and limitations of these after-school centers. Chapter 5 analyzes the potential of structured programs, focusing on a case study of a psychoeducational program for early adolescent girls. Although fidelity of implementation left much to be desired, the program enhanced the mentoring potential of staff leaders for girls struggling with a wide range of psychosocial issues accompanying puberty. Chapter 6 examines the battle waged between girls and boys over the use of the gym. A 3-year account of this struggle at one club highlights the obstacles as well as some solutions. We also consider more broadly how the focus on gender differences, rather than similarities, limited opportunities for both girls and boys.

The conclusion, chapter 7 presents a plan for how to improve typical, garden-variety after-school programs of this type. I present specific suggestions for how these sites can enhance relationship development while incorporating some of the strengths of more structured programs. Particular attention is devoted to reconciling the informal culture of these centers with the more formal specifications of structured programming. Policy implications of the mentoring findings are considered.

NOTES

1. National Research Council and Institute of Medicine (2002); Noam & Miller (2002).

2. The nature of after-school programs and developmental gains has been conceptualized in a variety of ways. For example, see Benson (1997); Carnegie Corporation of New York (1992); Connell, Gambone, & Smith (2000); Hawkins, Catalano, & Associates (1992); Pittman & Wright (1991); Pittman, Irby, & Ferber (2000); Quinn (1999).

3. Charles Stewart Mott Foundation (1998); Metropolitan Life (1994).

4. Paikoff & Brooks-Gunn (1991).

5. Cuban (1992); Eccles, Midgley, Wigfield, Buchanan, Reuman, & Flanagan, et al. (1993); Lipsitz (1984).

6. Hirsch & Rapkin (1987).

7. Damon (1995), p. 15.

8. See Belle (1999) for a fuller account of the familial context of after-school activities.

9. Heymann (2000).

10. Chase-Lansdale et al. (2003); Duncan & Chase-Lansdale (2001).

11. Boorman, Hewes, Overman, & Brown (2002).

12. The historical review draws heavily on Halpern (2003), though he does not address the increased attention to preventive interventions.

13. Personal communication, Irv Katz, President, National Assembly/National Collaboration for Youth, February 12, 2003.

14. Reiss (1989).

15. Little & Wynn (1989).

16. Halpern (2003), p. 4.

17. Cited in Halpern (2003), p. 93.

18. See National Research Council and Institute of Medicine (2002), p. 3.

19. Durlak & Wells (1997, 1998).

20. Catalano, Berglund, Ryan, Lonczak, & Hawkins (1999).

21. Gottfredson (2001).

22. The distinction is taken from the public health field.

23. Fashola (2002).

24. McLaughlin, Irby, & Langman (1994).

25. Halpern (1992); Halpern, Barker, & Mollard (2000).

26. Few of these studies have been subject to peer review.

27. The principal studies of Boys & Girls Clubs have been by Schinke and colleagues (Schinke, Cole, & Poulin, 2000; Schinke, Orlandi, & Cole, 1992) and by Public/Private Ventures (Arbreton & McClanahan, 2002; Gambone & Arbreton, 1997), and present positive findings about the value of the clubs.

28. Warren, Feist, & Nevárez (2002).

29. Dynarski et al. (2003). Supported by $1 billion in federal funds during fiscal year 2002, the Centers operated after-school programs in about 7,400 rural and inner-city public schools. The Bush administration had funneled the funds into block grants to the states and proposed to cut the funding severely, using the evaluation results as justification for the cutback. However, Congress voted not to reduce funding.

30. Cf. Lerner (1995).

31. Kaplan (1964), p. 293.

32. See Fine and Sandstrom (1988) for a discussion of some of the issues involved in doing ethnographic fieldwork with children.

33. Warren, Brown, & Freudenberg (1999)

34. Dynarski et al. (2003); Grossman et al. (2002); Walker & Arbreton (2001).

I

RELATIONSHIPS

2

HAVING FUN WITH FRIENDS:
A PLACE TO BE A KID

It can take an adult awhile to get acclimated to these types of youth settings. There are lots of young people and, often, a whirlwind of activities. As I was getting to know the clubs, one of the first things that struck me is that they are great places to have fun with friends. Friendships and recreation are not at the top of most researchers' and policymakers' list of priorities. However, by spending time with youth one can begin to appreciate that those factors play a critical role in program recruitment and retention—and no program will accomplish anything unless youth show up and keep showing up. So it is fitting to begin our report with this topic. To provide readers with an idea of what it is like in these clubs, to paint a portrait of its people and places and the centrality of recreation and relationships, I describe my experiences during one late afternoon. Later in the chapter, after weaving in findings from our survey questionnaire, I refer to this account to articulate a broader theoretical and practical understanding of the role of having fun with friends in the design of after-school programs.

> I am at the East Side Boys & Girls Club and can feel a headache coming on. The headache is not because of anything bad that is taking place— no one is giving me a hard time and things seem to be running smoothly. No, I am getting a headache because of all the noise. It can be very loud in the club, and especially so in the gym, where I am sitting. There are

23

a few dozen youth there and the hubbub is incessant. Some are running around with their friends, shouting as they go. Others are chatting along the side of the court, trying to make themselves heard above the general din. It makes for a lot of noise, particularly for a set of middle-aged ears. I know that if I were at home, and my children were making that much noise with their friends, at some point I would have enough, and tell them if they are going to be that loud, that they'll have to go outside. Yet no one tells them that here. They go on making a racket. And even though I'm getting a headache from it all, I smile, because it's clear that they're having a great time.

It's a large and attractive gym. I have a good view sitting up in the bleachers, about six or seven rows up. The ceiling is very high and there are a few dozen high-intensity lamps shining down on the wood floor. Only one of the lamps is not working. There are two glass backboards for basketball at either end of the court and they are clean and in good shape. The basketball rims are not crooked or bent, as they are at many city playgrounds. There are lots of different activities going on simultaneously but, miraculously, no one group of youth intrudes too much, or for too long, on the space of any other group.

A group of older guys, about 15 or 16 years old, are playing basketball in front of me. They are mostly just shooting the ball around, not really playing a game. They practice their moves on each other, playing a little defense, but not too much, so that each guy has a decent chance to show off and make his shots. Occasionally one of the guys will get serious for awhile and they'll go at each other competitively, but it doesn't last long this evening. They are just having fun and giving each other the opportunity to do well.

A group of girls about 12 to 13 years old move to part of the court where the guys are playing basketball. The girls take up about one quarter of the court, as well as part of the sidelines, as they begin playing double Dutch. This is a form of jump rope, where there are two girls at each end of the rope. The rope itself is doubled over. The girls take turns jumping inside and making some sort of deliberate movement (e.g., turning around on one foot), while those swinging the rope sing a song. Sometimes a loose basketball comes their way; they just pick it up and throw it back. There is no problem, today, in sharing the space.

There are two groups of younger kids at the other end of the court. One group of guys about 7 or 8 years old are playing touch football. Some of the younger boys are playing competitively; others are taking it in a much more easygoing manner. One boy gets frustrated repeatedly, confronting and yelling at those on the other team. At some point, Charles, the sports director, has to step in and authoritatively calm things down. The football players share that end of the court with another group of boys and girls, about the same age, who are playing tag. The tag players run here and there, sometimes through the football players (who adjust to their presence as if in a dance), and once in awhile up into the bleachers. Being an adult, I worry that tag players are going to get hurt when they go into the bleachers with all the hard wood edges around but, today, there are no bumps or bruises.

Off the edge of that side of the court, Charles takes out some golf equipment and an artificial putting green. He demonstrates how to play and some guys and girls take turns practicing. The kids do this more shyly than anything else, with motions that are a bit awkward, suggesting that they don't have much experience in this activity. However, they are good-natured in trying things out.

Eventually, Charles puts the golf equipment away and comes over to where the early adolescent girls are hanging out (the jump rope having ended some time back). He starts talking to them about an upcoming sleepover at the club and tries to get them to sign up to attend. They swap stories about the last sleepover, who was there, what activities took place, who tried to get away with what. They smile and joke with each other while reminiscing and a few of the girls say that they'll come to the sleepover. As a few new girls join the group, two of them lean up against Charles and one of them puts her arm on his shoulder. Charles is about six feet tall, 30ish, muscular but relaxed, and he doesn't change his position when the girls make contact with him. He neither encourages nor discourages the contact, not responding in any way noticeable to my attentive glance. I have a few associations to this episode. I remember when I was about 7 or so, my friends and I every once in awhile would lean up against one of us and call the leaned-upon-one a PLP. This stood for "public leaning post," and this seems to me what Charles has become. The more intellectual part of my brain thinks back to the philosopher Jean-Paul Sartre's description of a woman and a man in a café.[1] When the man reaches over and touches the woman's hand, she acts as if the hand was not part of her body, but rather was another object, like a cigarette. With this response, she does not acknowledge any romantic possibility suggested by the physical contact. Charles appears to take a similar tack to the innocent and very mild flirtations of these young adolescent girls. He stands there and continues chatting, a PLP, not responding physically, an asexual but friendly presence.

Charles checks his watch and remembers that the gym needs to be set up for a special event later that evening. So he recruits some of the teen guys to bring out and set up about a dozen round tables. As he leaves the gym, however, the guys just continue to play ball. Coming back a few minutes later, he yells at them to get going with the tables. As he stays in the gym this time, the guys start taking out the tables, making sure that the tables are set up OK, but not displaying much enthusiasm for the task. Typical teenagers, I think to myself, doing their chores.

The gym is not always like this. Sometimes the basketball games are very competitive. Sometimes the boys and girls are unwilling to share the floor. Yet today is not unusual.

Proceeding down a long hall, I find a number of teenage girls on the computer. They go to different sites on the Web, and talk with each other about what they are finding. At the side of the room, Cheryl, a woman in her mid-30s, is filling out some paperwork. She greets me with her great smile, beaming all this good will out at you. We chat for awhile and then Cheryl greets a teenage girl who hasn't been to the club recently, giving her that same big smile. I walk around the room. I notice Cheryl has a schedule up specifying what activity takes place during each period of the afternoon and evening. I look at my watch and notice that the designated activity is not taking place, does not appear to have just ended, and does not appear about to begin. This is not unusual, as meetings often do not take place as scheduled, although the groups do exist and do meet.

As I return to the gym, I talk with one of my research assistants about our sense of the club. We try to come up with some words to capture what the club is like, but no analogy is perfect. In some ways, it's like a great playground during warm weather, with loads of kids running around having a great time. Except that right now it's wintry cold and no kids anywhere use playgrounds when the temperature is this frigid. Moreover, playgrounds in high-crime communities such as the one where the club is located are just not safe places. That's where gangs loiter and drugs are peddled.[2] Playgrounds also don't have computers and art classes and other organized activities and trips. And they are unlikely to have the regular, safe presence of older, aunt- and uncle-type figures, keeping things under control and handing out plentiful quantities of warmth, support, and guidance. We return to a notion that our research group has talked about, of the club being a second home. There are good reasons why we, and many of the kids, consider the clubs a second home (see next chapter), but these mostly have to do with the warmth of the relationships in the club, not the physical space. I have seen only one or two homes of this physical size, and only as a tourist visiting what had formerly been mansions of the very wealthy.

Our reflections are interrupted as kids swirl around us. My now throbbing headache reminds me that whatever label we may try to pin on this club, it is clear that it is a great place to have fun with your friends. This may not seem to be such a striking or important claim if you live in a community in which such places are abundant. However, in these urban neighborhoods, it is a rare place indeed.[3] The streets are unsafe and the schools are unfriendly. At home, you may have responsibilities, such as taking care of younger children. So the youth center is a place where, quite simply, you can be a kid.

Alex Kotlowitz, in a deservedly well-known book, made the claim, reflected in the book's title, that "there are no children here."[4] He argued that inner-city children were exposed to too much violence, death, and hardship to be able to have what we would think of as a childhood. And all of those factors exist for these youth, as will be seen. However the youth center is a place where these troubles and cares can, for the most part, be put aside. They can act silly and goofy here. They can run around and yell. They can play sports and games and just hang out with their friends. They can take a break from trying to do better at school, and learning and developing in this way and that, preparing for eventual adulthood. In this safe place, for a time they can just be kids, enjoying themselves and life as children.

The adult staff at the club support this immersion in the satisfactions of childhood. The adults give them permission to have fun with their friends. It is clear that most of the adults recognize that the time that youth spend just simply enjoying themselves is of intrinsic worth. It is a youth identity or way of being in the world that these adults value and appreciate. Yes, the adults do want the children to learn and achieve, but having time to have fun is important too. The adult staff are important as well because part of a good childhood is having warm and caring adults around to be part of life. The staff supply this important ingredient in abundance.

Historically, having fun with friends in unstructured activities and being involved with caring adults have been characteristic of low-income African American youth.[5] It has become increasingly difficult to enjoy such a lifestyle, given the violence that pervades many of these communities. The clubs provide a setting that is culturally consonant with this pattern, while supplementing it with more structured activities.

Friendships involve more than fun. They have a special resonance in the lives of adolescents. A more careful look at these relationships is needed to understand more fully the importance of peer ties in the clubs and the implications they have for the design of urban after-school programs.

THE YOUTH CENTER AS A PLACE FOR FRIENDSHIP

Over the past 2 decades, the social sciences have increasingly recognized the importance of friendship to the development of adolescents.[6] Friendship provides opportunities for learning about the world, for exploring identity, for problem solving and social support. The intensity of adolescent friendship can help teens transition from reliance on parents to autonomy and independence. As Elizabeth Douvan and Joseph Adelson noted in one of the first large-scale studies of friendship:

> The particular advantage of the adolescent friendship is that it offers a climate for growth and self-knowledge that the family is not equipped to offer, and that very few persons can provide for themselves. Friendship engages, discharges, cultivates, and transforms the most acute passions of the adolescent period, and so allows the youngster to confront and master them. Because it carries so much of the burden of adolescent growth, friendship acquires at this time a pertinence and intensity it has never had before nor (in many cases) will ever have again.[7]

If friendships are indeed important to youth, and if the clubs are an important setting for friendship, then friendship ought to play an important role in how youths experience the club.

At this point, my inclination would be to turn to review the social science literature on the salience of peer ties to youth experience in the clubs. Unfortunately, I could find no prior study that has focused on this issue. To address this gap and explore the role of peer ties in these settings, Tondra Loder and I decided to study friendships of girls at two different clubs.[8] These girls were members of two different girls-only programs: Smart Girls (n = 6 girls) at the West River Club and Positive Girls (n = 11 girls) at the New City Club. The girls ranged in age from 10 to 15 (mean = 12 years old). Studying friendships of girls in club programs allowed us to examine the potential linkage between peer ties and program development.[9]

The first question we addressed was whether the girls had close friendships at the club. During individual interviews, we asked the girls to draw a map of kids with whom they hang out at the club or outside of the club. They were asked to put their own initials in the center of the page, and then place the initials of close friends near their own initials, and those of their *associates* (the term they used to refer to casual acquaintances) toward the edge of the paper. I had developed this procedure many years before and found, with both adolescents and adults, that it provided a participatory and satisfying method for assessing social networks.[10] The girls were then asked a series of questions about each friend and rated the closeness of each friendship on a 1–5 scale.

The girls placed an average (mean) of 18 peers on their maps. Of these, more than half attended the same club. Among the innermost circle of closest friends on their map, 74% attended the club. On our 1–5 rating scale, girls gave the highest closeness rating possible (= 5) to 59% of their club friends. In addition, 76% stated that their best friend was a member of their girls-only group. Thus, across assessment procedures, the data indicate that the girls had many close friends at the club.

The importance of the youth center to girls' friendships is underscored when we compare peer ties in the club with those in schools or the neighborhood more generally. During the interview, girls referred repeatedly to the freedom they had to interact in the club as contrasted with the other settings. As Nikita, a 12-year-old Positive Girl told us, "[W]ell, if we talk at school, the teacher will tell you to be quiet and give you detention. Outside [in the neighborhood], people will try to fight you." This was seconded by Dominique, another Positive Girl, who commented that "in school, because we're in different grades, it makes it hard for us to pass messages back and forth to each other. The teacher tells you to be quiet. Get back in line. So we meet in the washroom."

The values that friends support are important as well. It is good that youth have close friends at the club. It would also be good to know that these friendships are supportive of positive values. Much of the social science literature has focused on how peers can exert peer pressure in support of gang involvement and teen pregnancy, and in opposition to academic success.[11] Attention to how peers can be used to promote positive behaviors has increased in recent years.[12] There is no question that the girls we spoke to know peers in their neighborhood who have the potential to be negative influences: A quarter of the Positive Girls, for example, identified girls in their peer network who had already dropped out of elementary school. The Positive Girls wanted little to do with these dropouts: "They into too much stuff. They smoke, they ain't enrolled in school. They just out there." By contrast, the girls indicated that their club friends did better in school, didn't get into trouble, and were more serious about what they did. Even when the differences between good and bad influences are seen as more nuanced, the differences can be enough to enable girls to cope successfully. As Dominique said of her close friends,

> They do the same things I do. People aren't stuck up or self-centered. We don't drink and do drugs. Well, some of them drink, but they don't encourage other people to do it. Some of them smoke weed, but they don't encourage other people to do it.

Thus, these youth centers provide an environment where girls can develop friendships that are not only close, but that also, on balance, seem to support positive values. Youth who want to avoid negative behaviors appear able to find close friends at the club who will support that lifestyle.

RECRUITMENT, RETENTION, AND PROGRAM IMPLEMENTATION

Given the closeness of many of their peer relationships at the club, it made sense to examine the role that these ties may have played in getting the girls to come to the club—that is, recruitment. Friendships indeed played an important role in attracting them to the club, as girls indicated that they came to the club initially because of peers (42%), a parent (47%), or club activities (24%). Most of the girls (71%) came to the club with same-age peers, whether their siblings, friends, or kin (e.g., cousins).

Friendship also played a critical role in retention. Girls reported that friendships were the main draw that kept them coming to the club (53%), more so than was the case for either activities (35%) or adult staff (12%). It is important to note, moreover, that when girls referred to activities as an important reason why they kept coming to the club, they had in mind the kind that were done with peers.

We also examined the comparative importance of fun activities with friends in a survey questionnaire administered to 300 youth in the four clubs we studied during Year 1 of the research. In the survey, we asked both girls and boys to list their favorite activities. If fun with friends is a core attraction of these settings, that should be reflected here. Figure 2.1 reports the results of that query, broken down by activity type and gender. As can be seen, for the overwhelming majority of both girls and boys, physical activities were clearly the favorite, followed by games. Both of these types of activities were done entirely, or most frequently, with friends. Indeed, these are exactly the kinds of activities that were frequently punctuated by the loud sounds that gave me my headache. The survey findings indicate that these preferences are broad based and not idiosyncratic to members of the two girls-only programs. The overwhelming preference of both girls and boys for these types of activities provides strong support for considering the activities as a core feature of these types of settings.

Regarding the role of friendships in program implementation, at this point it should not be surprising to learn that friendships had an impact in this realm as well. At the New City Club, the Positive Girls had few opportunities to play around with each other and socialize. Few other activities were available for girls beyond the Positive Girls group. In the absence of other opportunities, the Positive Girls used the first part of their meeting to talk to and have fun with each other. Pat, the adult leader of the group, often had to struggle to engage the girls in formal programming. Pat usually spent the first half hour of meeting time gathering the girls up from the recreation room or gym. Once the session began, many of the girls continued to talk, joke, and roughhouse with each other, and often continued to do so throughout the meeting.

By contrast, many more activities were available for Smart Girls at the West River Club. Although the girls enjoyed and appeared to learn from the Smart Girls program, 82% of them indicated that their favorite activity was a recreational one. For most girls, this meant the club's double Dutch jump

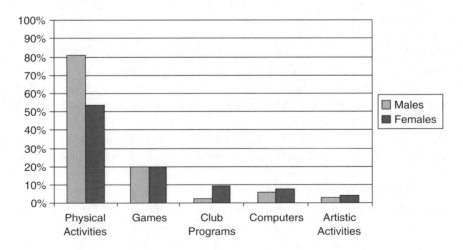

Figure 2.1. Youth's favorite activities.

rope team. They were able to participate in a range of physical and other activities at the club with their friends. The girls did not have to use Smart Girls to socialize, as they had many other venues to do so; the adult group leader was accordingly able to conduct the group in a much more orderly manner.

The finding that 82% of the Smart Girls preferred a recreational activity to a psychoeducational program provides additional support to the broader survey result on this issue. There was some question in our minds whether those survey results might reflect the fact that some of the clubs offered few formal programs, or formal programs that had only recently been launched. However, the West River Club had a number of popular programs, and Smart Girls was probably the best of these. The girls attended Smart Girls regularly and participated actively, and the adult leader was highly regarded. These findings suggest that even when recreational activities are compared with strong psychoeducational programs, the former will be preferred to the latter.

These varied findings converge to suggest that having fun with friends is a core motivation for participation in urban youth development organizations. This makes sense given the importance of friendships to adolescents, the priority given to friendships with fellow club members, and the extent to which youth enjoy the time they spend with their friends at the club. The importance of peer friendships has often been underestimated. Instead, we suggest that youth after-school programs should assign high priority to providing diverse recreational programs. These types of programs are of great intrinsic satisfaction and they provide an unparalleled setting for the evolution of friendships. As a bonus, ties to adult staff often develop in this context as well. Once this key foundation has been put in place, psychoeducational programs can be implemented more effectively, as reflected in the differential operational experience of Smart Girls versus Positive Girls.

RESPECT FOR ADOLESCENTS
AND ADOLESCENCE

My thesis is not merely that program developers ought to attend to peer dynamics, which can be assented to readily enough, but that having fun with friends should be a core foundation of urban after-school programs. Practitioners and evaluators know that a strong peer climate is key to making an after-school program attractive.[13] But there is little theoretical justification for this claim and, without further discussion, it is unlikely to strike a chord among policymakers. So I will switch gears somewhat now and consider the supporting arguments.

A focus on fun and friends is not the first thing that pops into one's head when thinking of poor urban youth. Quite the contrary, much academic and policy discourse focuses on programs designed by highly educated professionals that teach youth academic and interpersonal skills— skills that the youth do not have but need to keep them from dropping out of school, becoming pregnant, engaging in violent behavior, and so on. These, indeed, are serious issues, and a focus on fun seems decidedly out of place. Why should social policy pay for children to have a place to have fun with their friends, when there are such other, more pressing concerns?

Such a view would be familiar to some of the executives with leadership positions in this Boys & Girls Clubs regional affiliate. The data we found on the importance of recreational activities were not entirely new to them. When they visited the clubs, they heard much the same thing. Yet the executives did not act on this knowledge and never quite knew what to do with it. It seemed markedly inconsistent with their hopes to leave behind the "gym and swim" tag that is part of the Clubs' legacy. Making more room for games and sports was not a strategy that seemed designed to lead them toward their hope of becoming known as a more professional social service agency that could address a wide range of policy objectives.[14]

So let us consider the arguments in favor of making fun with friends a core foundation of urban after-school programs. Each argument will find favor with some potential constituency.

The Baby-Sitting Argument

For some, the most important function of after-school programs is to keep high-risk youth off the streets and away from problem behavior. When they are at the program site, youth are not engaging in violence, getting pregnant, or using drugs. The more time that youth spend in supervised after-school settings, the less time they have for problem behaviors. Thus, effectively, after-school programs provide society with baby-sitting services to keep high-risk youth out of trouble.

From this perspective, fun with friends should be a core foundation of after-school programs because, pragmatically, that is what draws youth to these settings and keeps them there. The most important function of club activities, accordingly, is recruitment to and retention in the site. The activities themselves should not be illegal, unethical, or contrary to prevailing social values, a test that fun with friends appears to pass easily at these sites. If that test is passed, pragmatism rules, and if recreational activities appear to be what best gets them to the site, then so be it.

One interesting, longitudinal study bears discussion as at first glance it might appear to question whether fun with friends actually does pass the above-mentioned test. Joseph Mahoney, Hakan Stattin, and David Magnusson reported a longitudinal study that examined the criminal behavior of 13-year-old Swedish boys who participated in recreational settings.[15] They found that participation was associated with increased likelihood of criminal behavior during adolescence and adulthood. However, as the authors noted, the Swedish centers differed in important ways from many other after-school programs, including the types we studied in this research. In contrast to the sites we studied, the Swedish centers involved little interaction with adult staff and few opportunities for skill development. Although the effect sizes were quite small and the study was correlational rather than experimental, these findings do suggest caution about designing after-school programs that focus exclusively on recreational activities in a peer-only context. However, my thesis is that fun with friends should be a foundation for such programs, not the exclusive focus.

Those who are drawn to the baby-sitting argument tend to be suspicious, or at least cautious, about claims that the programs themselves produce preventive effects above and beyond their baby-sitting function. Advocates of such a position may not be willing to fund recreational activities for reasons of intrinsic value, but could do so for pragmatic, extrinsic reasons.

The Instrumental–Developmental Argument

For most of those who work with youth, and many of those who pass judgment on youth programs, one of the most critical functions of after-school programs is to provide youth with the knowledge, attitudes, and skills that promote successful development in adolescence and prepare them well for adult life. The developmental potential of the program is typically conceived as a function of the quality of the adult mentoring as well as the effectiveness of formal programs and activities.

From this perspective, fun with friends provides a foundation because, instrumentally, it draws youth to the site and facilitates their involvement in developmentally enhancing activities and relationships. This way of thinking shares with the baby-sitting advocates a very pragmatic approach to fun with friends. Both emphasize the instrumental function of recreation in drawing youth to the site. Those in the instrumental–developmental camp believe that adult relationships and formal programs have important benefits whereas the baby-sitting advocates are skeptical of those claims. The former see recreation as a vehicle to draw youth into other relationships and activities at the site, whereas the latter see recreation as an alternative to problem behaviors outside of the site.

The instrumental–developmental group is engaging in a type of marketing that has its parallel in the commercial world. Bait and switch, for example, refers to a tactic in which an inexpensive item is used to attract customers who are then encouraged to purchase a similar but more expensive item. Businessmen also use loss leaders, attractive items priced below-cost to draw in customers, who will then purchase other, more profitable items. In the context of urban after-school programs, recreation can be seen as the draw for youth, who are then enticed into participating in adult mentoring and formal program activities.[16]

In order for this maneuver to work, adult staff need to have some sympathy for recreation and unstructured youth activities. They need to have some knowledge and comfort with those activities. By demonstrating these qualities to youth, young people are more likely to identify with the adults, see them as "cool," and respond positively when those adults engage them in dialogue about other issues or recruit them to participate in other activities led by these adults.

In the instrumental–developmental approach, adult staff join with youth in taking a sympathetic approach to youth culture.[17] This approach is different from that usually taken to youth culture in either social science research or social policy. Beginning with James Coleman's work on high school students, many have decried youth's attraction to "the superficial values of a hedonistic culture" and have sought ways to squash or subvert it.[18] By contrast, the type of after-school program we studied finds ways to sympathize with some central values of that culture, such as friendship, informality, expressiveness, music, athletics, games, and so on. These positively valued aspects are given time and space to flourish. Other tendencies of the culture, such as violence, are expressly disapproved of and prohibited. Adult staff limit the time allocated to unstructured activities and then channel youth into developmentally enhancing activities. Even in these latter activities, however, skillful staff draw on aspects of youth culture, such as informality, expressiveness, and the desire of friends to be together, to engage youth in the activity.

Thus, positive features of the youth's environment and culture are drawn on and, in important ways, replicated in the club setting. In this way, this type of after-school program provides a bridge between youth's natural social environments and the adult world, creating similar processes as a means to first engage and then socialize youth.

The instrumental–developmental argument accordingly provides two reasons for paying for youth to have fun with friends. The first, similar to the baby-sitting argument, is that such activities draw youth to the site. Once there, they can be engaged in mentoring relationships and skill-enhancing activities that increase the likelihood of positive adolescent and adult outcomes. Second, having fun with friends can be used in mentoring and formal programs themselves, more fully engaging youth and thereby potentially increasing program effectiveness.

The Intrinsic Value Argument (Weak Version)

We now turn to two arguments that focus on the intrinsic worth of recreation and having fun with friends. I consider the first of these to be a weak version insofar as the claims are more narrow and the argument less complex.

Many adults talk fervently of getting youth involved with activities other than drugs and sex. They would like to see youth enjoy themselves in ways that are not in opposition to adult values. The criterion here appears to be activities that could be classified as wholesome or as good-natured fun. The kind of friendship interactions described earlier in this chapter would seem to be exactly this kind of activity. The children chat with their friends, play games, toss the ball around, learn about golf, spend time on the computer, and talk with adults. At these youth clubs, this alternative exists and the youth are drawn to it. They have good old-fashioned fun with their friends. This is as innocent as it is likely to get.

Although the logic of this argument may have appeal to some, I might caution those who are sympathetic that the wholesomeness might not be immediately evident were they to visit one of these types of youth sites. Instead, what will make the most immediate impression is the whirlwind of activity, with groups of teens moving about quickly and loudly—in a word, chaos. Things have the potential to get out of hand at any such site, and did for a time at the New City Club during the second year of our research, when funding was restricted in anticipation of building a new club in the same general neighborhood. However, mostly, it is only the appearance of chaos to unknowing eyes (and an adult nervous system not inoculated with a prior dose of aspirin). As I sought to show in the first part of this chapter, beneath the veneer of chaos lie ordered patterns that permit but bound youthful energy.

This more conservative perspective has some similarities to the baby-sitting argument. For the baby-sitters, it is important that program activities not include any negative activities; the intrinsic value perspective demands a bit more—that the activities go beyond value-neutrality to represent some minimal level of positive value.

The Intrinsic Value Argument (Strong Version)

This version of the intrinsic desirability argument places great emphasis on children's culture. It is a perspective that is more complex and controversial than any of the prior positions. Part of the argument is based on an emerging body of literature, mostly but not entirely European, in the anthropology and sociology of childhood.[19]

From a developmental perspective, each of us grows up, leaving behind our childhood and adolescence. From a more structural, population perspective, however, there is always a large group of children and adolescents, even though its membership changes. This is true as well for the period of early adolescence, the principal emphasis of this book. Typically considered in modern societies to encompass the age range of 10 to 15, the ages of entrance into and exit from it vary. Nevertheless, unless there is some drastic, unforeseen biological or social change, for the foreseeable future we can expect that a large group of youth will be dealing with the joys and tribulations of early adolescence. In this way, early adolescents constitute a distinct group in society, even if its membership changes over time.

Early adolescents partake of a more general youth culture within our society. The culture reflects a particular orientation toward music, dance, and clothes, a preference for time spent hanging out with friends, flirtatiousness with possible romantic interests (often done so that genuine interest can be denied), and a host of other activities, done stylishly if possible. In youth culture, adolescents, not adults, are the experts. In this realm, the competencies of youth can be expressed and, often, admired. And, of course, in this realm having fun with friends is a core value.

A policy that provides space for the positive aspects of youth culture to flourish communicates respect for adolescents. It respects the culture of a group that is powerless, without political franchise, and unable to speak effectively for itself in the policy realm. Funding should not be restricted only to those activities that are designed to assimilate the marginal group into the dominant (i.e., adult) culture. It is necessary to protect the rights of marginalized groups, including adolescents, to retain their culture and to have places in which they are the competent ones, the experts.

If youth culture is taken away entirely, adolescents will be robbed of many of their competencies. Such a deficit orientation highlights their limitations and failures. Does anyone genuinely believe that such an approach makes it likely that they will follow adult advice and guidance?

Adults need to adopt a more respectful stance to what is important to youth. We, as adults, may not value recreation and friendship that highly, though it is worth remembering that Aristotle put friendship at the very center of his ethical philosophy.[20] What is clear is that having fun with friends is a fundamental aspect of the lives of young people. If we are to treat youth more seriously, then we need to accord respect to such preferences, especially as they are not discordant with adult values.

Here, then, is the beginning of an alternative discourse that dignifies youthful recreation and having fun with friends. Such a discourse is important to practice as well as to theory. Comprehensive youth settings, such as these clubs, are loath to diminish their recreational offerings; they realize that it is their bread and butter, but because it does not seem to be a very sophisticated realm, they are reluctant to embrace it. Advocates and youth leaders need a justification of recreation that is theoretically sophisticated. I hope that this work provides the initial steps in constructing a competing discourse that gives dignity and importance to fun with friends.[21]

CONCLUSION

This chapter has presented theory and empirical research findings on the importance of peer friendships in urban after-school programs. In contrast to the usual placement of peer ties in the background, I have argued that having fun with friends is a central feature and benefit of these programs. Indeed, peer ties play a major role in recruitment, retention, and program implementation.

A number of arguments were then considered for why policymakers should fund recreational components of urban after-school programs. Each argument has some merit and will appeal to some interested parties. If time or other constraints limited me to only one, I would offer the instrumental–developmental argument. It taps into widespread support for mentoring programs across political groups and has the largest potential payoff in terms of adolescent and adult outcomes.

Although the principal thesis of this chapter is that peer ties are fundamental to understanding and designing after-school programs, I do not wish to leave the reader with the impression that my view of peer ties is idyllic. As will be seen in the following chapters, much staff time is spent addressing interpersonal conflicts among youth and preventing confrontations from escalating into violence. Conflict, too, is an important way in which peer ties impact after-school programs. It does not, however, detract from the beneficial aspects of friendships described in this chapter. If anything, resolving tensions that might tear youth apart enables positive features of friendship to flourish and greatly enhances the meaningfulness of youth programs.

NOTES

1. Sartre (1966). See section on patterns of bad faith.
2. Flynn (1999).
3. Larson, Richards, Sims, & Dworkin (2001).
4. Kotlowitz (1991).
5. Lareau (2000).
6. Bukowski, Newcomb, & Hartup (1996); Savin-Williams & Berndt (1990); Way (1998); Youniss & Smollar (1985).
7. Douvan & Adelson (1966), p. 174.
8. A more detailed report of this research is provided in Loder and Hirsch (2003).
9. There were no statistically significant differences between these subsamples of girls and girls from those clubs more generally on a wide range of demographic, school, and psychological variables.

10. The procedure was adapted from Hirsch (1980).

11. Anderson (1989); Brunswick & Rier (1995); Campbell (1991); Fordham & Ogbu (1986); Huff (1990).

12. Cowie (1999); Lerner (1995); Peterson & Rigby (1999); Salmivalli (1999); Turner (1999).

13. Dynarski et al. (2003); Warren et al. (2002). The NYC Beacons appeared to have been successful in making the setting an attractive place for friendship. The evidence from the 21st Century Community Learning Centers evaluation, although indirect, suggests that the Centers were not so successful in this regard (e.g., sparse attendance rates, students in the comparison group indicating that they would be more likely to attend the Centers if their friends went there).

14. See Halpern (2003) for a historical account of identity issues facing urban after-school programs.

15. Mahoney, Stattin, & Magnusson (2001). The authors also fail to discuss that youth center participation was assessed during the year 1968, which was a time of vast social and political upheaval among youth. In this context, center participation may have played a very different role in youth life than during less tumultuous times.

16. Le Menestrel, Bruno, and Christian (2002) refer to sports as a "hook" that leads youth to participate in other activities to which they might not be initially drawn.

17. I take the term *joining* from the family therapy literature.

18. Coleman (1961), p. 55.

19. James, Jenks, & Prout (1998); James & Prout (1997); Qvortrup, Bardy, Sgritta, & Wintersberger (1994); Stephens (1995); Thorne (1993).

20. See Books VIII and IX of the *Nicomachean Ethics* (McKeon, 1941).

21. For some who advocate this type of perspective on children's culture, the 1989 UN Convention on the Rights of the Child provides important support (United Nations General Assembly, 1989). The Convention is an important document overseas among child specialists and nongovernmental organizations. There is little American discussion or even knowledge of it (though see Limber & Wilcox, 1996; Melton, 1991), despite the fact that the United States actively participated in the drafting of the Convention—attending every meeting of the working group leading up to the final draft—under the presidencies of political conservatives Ronald Reagan and George H. Bush. Indeed, the United States was heavily involved in drafting the two articles that are relevant to this chapter (the historical, legislative record is documented by Detrick, 1992; see also Cantwell, 1992; LeBlanc, 1995).

    The principal section of the Convention that bears on recreation is Article 31, paragraph 1, which recognizes "the right of the child to rest and leisure, to engage in play and recreational activities appropriate to the age of the child and to participate freely in cultural life and the arts." Additional support for this right is found in its conceptual linkage to other parts of the Convention that emphasize the importance of personality development and well-being (preamble, articles 3, 17, 24, 27, 29), the best interests of the child (article 3), social and cultural rights (article 4), and freedom of expression (article 12). The UNICEF handbook for the implementation of the Convention (UNI-CEF, 1998) makes clear that the types of activities that the article has in mind are very much those we have observed in our research sites. Article 31 does not preclude academically oriented after-school activities, even highly structured ones. But it treats leisure and recreation as protected classes of activity. Academic programs cannot replace or leave insufficient time for leisure and recreation.

The right of children to have their views taken seriously in matters such as leisure and recreation is given strong support in Article 12, paragraph 1, of the UN Convention:

> State Parties shall assure to the child who is capable of forming his or her own views the right to express those views freely in all matters affecting the child, the views of the child being given due weight in accordance with the age and maturity of the child.

With respect to engaging in recreational activities with friends, there appears to be little doubt that early adolescents are quite capable of forming their own views and, given sufficient age and maturity in these matters, to have their views given serious weight in decision making in after-school programs. Given that youth have repeatedly expressed their strong preference for recreational activities of the sort done primarily with friends, compliance with this article necessitates that significant time and resources be allocated to support those activities.

3

A SECOND HOME

While spending time in the clubs we heard numerous youth spontaneously refer to the club as a home or talk about the staff members as family. In fact, hanging out at the clubs, even as adult researchers, we often felt the warmth and hominess that emanated from the space. We began to consider studying the club as a second home; what ultimately clinched our decision to do so was our encounter with Sammy in the club library filling out his application for Youth of the Year.

In the application, Sammy, on his own initiative, emphasized that the club was his second home. It is instructive to note what qualities made the club such a place for him. He wrote that it is a "quiet space to do work, place to bond with friends, place to get away from peer/family pressure, place to confide in adults, safe space to get off the streets." What is most important is the range of supports that the club provides for him. He continues this theme by writing that the club "allows me to express myself mentally, verbally, physically and artistically." Indeed, Sammy enjoys a variety of physical activities at the club, such as swimming and weight lifting, and also is a good student who uses club time to do homework, hang out in the art and computer rooms, and baby-sit for younger club members to earn money to support the club activities in which he participates. The construction of a

---

This chapter is coauthored by Nancy Deutsch.

self or identity is a fundamental task of adolescence, and Sammy uses the club as a place to try out a rich variety of possible selves and see how they fit together. As Sammy noted in his application, the club is a place to express himself and put his "self-image in perspective." The club can be a home for many different parts of who he is. As shall be seen, Sammy's experience is far from unique.

THE IMPORTANCE OF PLACE

When people think back on their own childhoods, most of them can name a place in which they felt particularly comfortable or with which they felt a strong bond. Whether that place was the home of a favorite relative, a room in one's own home, or under a particular tree in a park, that place marked a special territory in which one felt "at home." It was a place one could go to get in touch with oneself, to cheer oneself up, to feel good. Yet, though many people can name such a place and perhaps provide vague reasons for why it was important, it is much harder to articulate the process by which one became attached to the place and through which it impacted one's life and identity.

Fortunately, there is an emerging body of theory and research on the importance of place in people's lives. The contributors to this literature come from an unusually wide range of disciplines, from psychology to geography to urban planning to landscape architecture. This literature attends to the individual meanings of important places and how those places impact individual identity and self-esteem. Individuals' bonds with environments have been studied as entities in their own right. There has even been suggestion of a separate place-identity that contributes to one's overall sense of self.[1]

Qualities of a social setting, such as emotional support, involvement, independence, organization and control, and physical comfort, impact people's functioning and development.[2] Settings that do not provide opportunities that fit adolescents' developmental needs can lead to negative psychological changes.[3] Indeed, urban youth may be attracted to gangs because they meet specific needs that are not being met by the youth's larger environment, such as a sense of belonging, companionship, safety, status, a loyal support system, and self-worth.[4] Youth organizations have the potential to offer similar qualities in a more positive environment.

PLACES, HOME–PLACES, AND IDENTITY

Environmental psychologists have coined the term *place attachment* to name the special emotional bond that an individual forms with a particular space.[5] Important places in people's lives provide them with security and stimulation, ties to others, and linkages to social institutions and culture.[6] The comfort found there can also help them cope with threats to sense of balance, unity, or self-esteem.[7]

Some theorists have suggested that attachment to home is a particularly important form of place attachment and that appropriation of a home-place is a universal and vital process that is essential to psychological well-being and a foundation of our identities.[8] A home can provide continuity for an individual over time through patterns of repetition and recurring activities. It may represent important relationships in the person's life and reflect cultural values to which the individual subscribes.[9] The home may also be a place where one is able to resist negative cultural stereotypes or oppression experienced within the larger society.[10] An imposed space is unlikely to be experienced as a home unless it is congruent with the individual's culture, values, preferences, and needs.[11]

Because adolescence is the time when youth separate from their families and begin to explore their own independence and identities outside their familial homes,[12] the desire for new, supportive spaces may be particularly strong during these years. Adolescents, as they begin to explore the larger environment outside their families, may feel a need for places that still reflect the values of their families and provide similar support, but that also allow them to develop an identity separate from their family. Attachment to a home-place, therefore, may fill a need for alternate environments that adolescents seek out as augmentations to their family.

As youth expand the number and types of social environments in which they move, they may find themselves occupying different social roles in different contexts. A variety of social roles across environments can be a positive, motivating force for youth and provide examples of possible selves that youth may explore and to which they may aspire. If the various roles are conflicting, however, and the youth cannot integrate the roles into a harmonious self-concept, differing roles may prove disturbing and even damaging.[13] For some minority and low-income groups, the social context of adolescence is characterized by ambiguous and often conflicting social roles. These youth may be expected to act as adults at home, by care-taking for younger siblings or working to assist the family financially, but be treated as children in school. This situation results in a conflict between familial and societal expectations and self-attributes.[14]

Social supports are important in helping adolescents bridge these potentially conflicting roles.[15] Most social contexts in which adolescents move tend to bring one role or identity domain to the forefront (e.g., academic or student role in school, caretaker at home, confidant or buddy with friends). Comprehensive after-school centers can act as sites for the integration of social roles. They provide a setting in which youth like Sammy can simultaneously enact multiple social roles. Youth can act childlike and athletic when playing sports, but also be responsible workers or caretakers by helping out with the younger kids. Staff members, in turn, can actively support adolescents' multiple and changing social roles through their responses to youth across these varied activities. Receiving support from an adult for these varied roles can provide a crucial foundation for identity integration.[16] A home-place that embeds multiple social roles and supports may provide youth with the space they need to address the developmental concerns associated with identity formation.

A home-place, then, is not necessarily one's familial home or place of residence. It is a place that is specified by the individual. A home-place provides a means for self-regulation and identity maintenance as well as empowerment. Appropriation of such a home, one that is linked to both the individual self and the community, may have special significance for urban youth living in poverty.

THE CLUB AS HOME

Analyzing the clubs not just as a place, but as a home–place, provides the tools necessary to hone place attachment theory to the types of urban after-school programs that we studied. A home is more than a place. If a space is transformed into a place through personal meaning, then a place is further transformed into a home through characteristics that imbue it with deeper personal significance. Through connections with the physical neighborhood in which these youth organizations are located, relations with staff and other children, activities that promote self-expression, and memories of childhood years at the clubs, adolescents may develop an attachment to these settings that helps to support their identities and self-esteem.

Although this way of conceptualizing the clubs fit with initial findings from our field research and was attractive theoretically, we were aware that little prior research focused specifically on the sense of place among adolescents. Existing studies of adolescent place attachment have focused on either private spaces, such as bedrooms or secluded spots in woods, or large, shared public spaces, such as areas within a World's Fair.[17] There had been only one study of home–places among poor, urban youth.[18] In this context, we believed it important to determine whether a representative sample of club youth consider the club to be a home–place, and to let them tell us in their own words why they did or did not experience the site in this way.

Accordingly, we incorporated a series of questions on the club as a possible home–place into interviews we conducted as part of our overall research. Members of the research team interviewed a total of 112 adolescents across the four clubs we studied during the first year of the research. This main interview sample is half boys, 59% African American and 41% Hispanic, with most youth coming from low-income families (86% receive free or reduced-price lunch at school) and single-parent households (60%). They ranged in age from 10 to 18, but most were in early adolescence, with an average age (mean) of 13.

As part of the interview, youth were told that "some kids have described the club as a second home to them. Other kids do not seem to think of the club as a home" and were asked whether they would describe the club as a home. If they reported that they considered the club a second home, they were then asked, "What makes it feel like a home to you?"

We suspected, on the basis of our observations, that a good number of youth would say that they felt the club was a home. We were not prepared, however, for the results to show such a strong majority of youth feeling that way. A full 74% of the youth interviewed said that they felt the club was a home. Boys and girls were equally likely to report that the club was a home, and there were no statistically significant age or race differences. There was, however, a marginally significant site difference, with one of the four clubs having a higher proportion of youth who thought of the club as a home. No club, however, had less than 61% of youth who thought of the club as a home. At the club with the highest percentage, 89% of youth called it a home.[19]

The fact that three quarters of youth who attend the clubs said that they would call their club a home is a tremendous testament to the success of these settings at creating a safe and inviting place for youth. The leaders of many organizations are prone to talk about how they are all like family there, or like a home. However, that is often just the boss talking for public relations purposes. Everyone else might feel rather differently. In the case of the clubs, however, it appears they got it right.

This finding should not be taken as a blanket endorsement of these types of youth settings. We are not Pollyannish about either the clubs or familial homes. Let us be clear: No club is perfect and every family and home provides negative as well as positive experiences. If we learned anything from Freud, it is that our experiences are often ambivalent. In this context, these youth nevertheless were able to select and emphasize the positive features of a familial home. They then used their cognitive–emotional response to those familial virtues to foster a connection to a kindred but nonfamilial setting. This is a crucial developmental skill. At a time of life full of contradictions, these young adolescents found a way to mobilize their positive experiences to cross a bridge into the nonfamilial world.

Yet we still did not have the answer to how the clubs got it right, the kinds of experiences that they successfully tapped. Many aspects of a space could contribute to thinking of it as a home. Positive childhood memories of home are likely made up of a combination of the physical surroundings and emotional qualities associated with the space. One may recall with fondness a favorite pillow or the color of the kitchen walls as well as love and support from family members or relaxation in front of the television. What is it about the club that make youth feel at home there? That is the core of the question we wanted to address.

In an attempt to answer this question we examined the youth's open-ended answers as to why they felt that the club was a home. Because we were interested in the relative importance of psychosocial versus physical qualities, we first coded the responses into those two major categories. Psychosocial responses were those that referred to an emotional or affective state or to relationships with others. Physical responses were those that referred to a specific physical characteristic of the club, such as furnishings, or to the club as a physical boundary from the outside world.

Perhaps it is not surprising that the vast majority of answers referred to psychosocial qualities of the club. Seventy-three percent of the youth reported at least one psychosocial reason for why they thought of the club as a home. The vast majority of these, 91%, referred to youths' interactions with other club members or staff. Sample psychosocial responses include the following:

> Like the people in here are nice and take care of you, they help you and sometimes let you do what you wanna do. I have a lotta friends.
> —Kathleen, 10-year-old Hispanic female

> The people care about you, you care about them . . . feel comfortable . . . come here and just hang loose, relax.
> —Frank, 16-year-old Hispanic male

> It feels safe . . . you don't have to worry about nothing.
> —Derek, 14-year-old African American male

> The way they surround you with all the little kids . . . feeling the happiness and smiling.
> —Tina, 15-year-old Hispanic female

> Everyone treats each other the same and it seems like they try to show a sense of comfort and love here . . . everyone sticks together and tries to love each other.
> —Latoya, 15-year-old African American female

> People here always listen to you and help you if you have problems, just like your parents, tell you what to do and what not to do so you won't get into trouble.
> —Judy, 11-year-old African American female

> The staff—they're always there for you like my parents. . . . There's nothing negative here, it's always positive.
> —Isaac, 16-year-old Hispanic male

As can be seen in these examples, feeling cared about by staff and seeing the adults as resources appeared to be of particular importance. An ability to come to the staff for help with problems on everything from homework to family issues was noted as key by a number of respondents. The emotional state associated with being at the club (e.g., happy, loved, relaxed) also played a role in youths' describing the club as a home. Many of these emotional qualities are related to the youths' relationships with staff or other youth at the clubs. Youth talked about the importance of having friends to have fun with and talk to, having staff to confide in, and feeling a general sense of happiness and caring inspired by the social atmosphere created by the people at the club.

In contrast, only 13% of youth reported a physical reason for why the club was a home. Half of those responses mentioned safety. Few of these young people listed only physical reasons for why the club is a home, but many of those who did referred to the club as an alternative to the streets. Sample responses coded as physical include the following:

> When I'm indoors in my house nothing happens but sometimes shooting, but I'm safe here.
> —Jose, 14-year-old Hispanic male

> You get to sit down in certain areas, seats are comfortable.
> —Tyrone, 10-year-old African American male

> Better than streets or gangbanging.
> —Jonathan, 15-year-old Hispanic male

> Because it's clean.
> —Julie, 10-year-old Hispanic female

The club as a physical boundary from the outside world is implied in the references many youth make to the club keeping them out of trouble and away from gangs. Whereas this is an important aspect to consider in how the club may function as a home to youth, it is apparently much less significant in youths' descriptions of the club as a home than are the psychosocial aspects, especially relationships. Whereas the safety of the club initially helps draw children to it and perhaps even keeps them involved as adolescents, it may not have the same impact on their transformation of the club from an important place to a home-place as do the psychosocial aspects of the club.

Youth responses were further coded into four subcategories that emerged in the youths' answers: relationships, time, safety, and activities.[20] A response could be coded for any number of major categories and subcategories.[21] The subcategories provide additional insight into the qualities that transform a place into a home for these youth.

Relationships with peers and staff at the club are by far the most important aspect for a majority of the youth who see the club as a home. Two thirds of youth included relationships in their answer. Forty-two percent of those responses directly mentioned or implied staff. Many referred to feelings of being cared for by staff and more than half highlighted the support or advice they get from staff, including academic help. Approximately one quarter of the responses that were coded for relationships discussed the role of friends and other children at the club. In addition to those responses that specifically referred to peers, some responses that talked about activities implied the role of friends. Activities such as playing a game or having a sleepover implicitly assume the participation of friends.[22]

Nearly a third of youth mentioned activities in their answers as to why the club felt like a home.[23] The specific activity most frequently referred to was homework. General activities such as playing and helping with the children were also popular answers. No specific club programs or structured activities were mentioned as a reason the club feels like a home. The amount of time spent at the club (e.g.,"I come here every day" or "I've grown up here") was mentioned explicitly by less than 20% of respondents.

There were no gender, age, or race differences in the reasons for why the youth reported the club was a home. As will be shown in later chapters, relationships with adults proved to be as important for boys as for girls at the clubs, and to have positive benefits for both.

Extended Kin and Schools: Other Possible Home-Places

The important role of relationships in making the clubs a home for these inner-city youth may reflect the traditional role of extended families in African American and Hispanic cultures. A considerable amount of research across the social sciences has focused on kin networks among African Americans. Most Blacks brought to America were from West Africa. Despite differences in the social structure among villages and tribes, strong kinship systems dominated. As a strategy for dealing with the massive hardship and social dislocations of slavery, Blacks drew on these African kin models, adapted them to the American context, and used them for mutual aid and support. They continued to draw on them during the reconstruction period and afterward.[24] More recent anthropological studies have confirmed the continued importance of extended family systems for African Americans, particularly those in or near poverty.[25] Similar findings have also been obtained in quantitative studies of African American and Hispanic adolescents.[26]

Do club youth also find home-places among their kin? In interviews with 12 additional girls at two clubs not included in the initial research, we asked not only about whether or not the club was a home (10 out of 12 said yes) but also specifically whether they could think of another place that felt like a home. Two thirds of the girls said that a home of a relative (usually an aunt or a grandmother) felt like a home to them. The reasons they gave were similar to those given for why the club was a home. Responses included the following:

> My grandparents' house, because my grandma's like a second mom and my grandpa like a second father.
> —Wanda, 11-year-old Hispanic female

*My grandparents' house, because my aunt and uncle live there and we have a
lot of fun. It's fun being there.*
—Tina, 12-year-old Hispanic female

*My cousin's house, they treat me like I'm in my own house. Same things I do
in my house I do there. Have room, TV, computer.*
—Tiffany, 13-year-old African American female

Six girls also named a second relative's house at which they felt at
home. Their reasons for this feeling included the following:

*'Cause my grandma lives there. She cooks for me all my favorite food. She goes
shopping with me and we go to eat.*
—Tina, 12-year-old Hispanic female

*My aunt and uncle because they make sure that I'm okay when I sleep and I
get fed. They take me out and buy me stuff. I'm the only one who sleeps over
of her god children. I have my own room to myself.*
—Gloria, 11-year-old Hispanic female

*My aunt. In the weekends I go to their house and my aunt cooks us breakfast
in the morning and my house is 8 blocks away. I have friends over there and
my cousins invite me to places.*
—Suzanne, 11-year-old Hispanic female

Once again, the responses given by these girls about their relatives'
homes mirror many of the reasons that youth gave for why the club felt like
a home. Ties to both adults and peers (friends and cousins) were important.
Although some girls talked about physical characteristics (having their own
room or possessions), even those answers were typically tied to the people in
the space. In addition, there appeared to be a feeling of being special invoked
by many of the physical- or activity-related answers, such as being taken
shopping or being the only one to stay overnight.

School: A Different Experience

In contrast to the large number of girls who were able to point to an
extended family member's house that felt like a second home, only four of
the girls said that school felt like a home to them. This is not surprising,
given negative perceptions of the school environment in early adolescence
(the girls we interviewed ranged in age from 11 to 15). Jacquelynne Eccles
and colleagues have suggested that this negative experience of the school
environment may be a result of a mismatch between the developmental
needs of early adolescence and the provisions of the school. At a time when
youth need close relationships with both adults and other adolescents, they
interact with a greater number of teachers for shorter amounts of time. Although they seek opportunities to demonstrate their autonomy, their school
days are increasingly scheduled and ruled by the bell, with few chances to
freely choose activities. The stage-environment fit theory proposes that this

mismatch may actually lead to some of the negative psychological changes that commonly have been associated with adolescence, including declining academic performance and motivation, truancy, self-criticism, anxiety, and, at times, decreased self-esteem.[27]

The research on school environments is echoed by the voices of the youth we interviewed. Their reasons for why they felt that school was or was not a home reflect many of the developmental needs highlighted by researchers and demonstrate how those needs are not being met. Of the four girls who did think of school as a home, two girls mentioned the fact that they get fed at school, a fairly straightforward way in which school meets a need for them. A third girl said that her friends make it feel like a home, pointing to how she feels positive social support from her peers. Only one girl referred to teachers, mentioning "all the teachers that care for you."

This is in stark contrast to the answers girls gave to explain why school did not feel like a home. Responses included too much work, annoying teachers, and "it's like jail." In fact, many of the youth who said school was not a home listed the teachers or the principal as a central reason. The feeling of being locked in and of having little choice or freedom was also prevalent. Thus, the qualities that make the club feel like a home—a range of supportive adults, opportunities for self-expression—appear to be missing or to be experienced negatively by these girls in school. This is not to say that all teachers are perceived negatively; as chapter 4 shows, most youth were able to name a supportive adult at school, but there was a sense that most teachers were unsympathetic toward them.[28]

Calling a place a home likely involves both comparisons with other places where one feels at home and contrasts to settings where one does not feel at home. The club as a home-place was compared favorably with the homes of their extended kin, with much overlap in the qualities that made these two types of settings homes to the youth. Schools, however, provided a clear contrast to the clubs for nearly all the girls. The girls contrasted qualities of the environment, such as social support, that were experienced positively at their families' homes and at the club, to their experiences at school.

The importance of aspects of the environment, particularly autonomy and social support, on adolescents' perceptions of place is further emphasized by the responses of girls who were asked where they felt most like themselves, at school or at the Boys & Girls club. Most of the girls said that they felt more like themselves at the club. Their reasons included the following:

> 'Cause I can express myself and have fun. Don't have to stay still.
> —Brandesha, 13-year-old African American female

> I express myself more at the club. I speak my mind. I'm not afraid to say what I say. In school you get in trouble. I can say anything here, speak my mind. I'm more myself.
> —Tiffany, 13-year-old African American female

I know people at the club better than I know people at school.
—Nikia, 13-year-old African American female

Similarly, at the NYC Beacons, 89% of youth reported that they always or often feel like they can be themselves there.[29]

We then asked the girls how they would feel if the club were to become more like school. Many said that they would stop coming to the club. One of those girls summed it up by saying, "I have to put up with a lot of it at school and I want to come to a fun place."

Given what girls had to say about their school experiences, it is not surprising that they reacted so negatively to this hypothetical situation. Many youth development organization leaders actually see the role of their programs as providing an alternative or antidote to schools.[30] It would be a mistake to assume that these negative school experiences are limited to those attending urban youth clubs (a selection bias among club participants). Negative reactions are widespread not only among urban youth, but also among students in nonurban schools with considerable resources.[31] In fact, researchers who have sought to study middle schools with the goal of identifying a positive model to follow have had considerable difficulty finding such schools, regardless of where they look.[32] Parents, too, in low-income communities frequently resent schools that have not served their children well.[33]

Nonetheless, current policy options include the possibility of expanding school into after-school hours, of turning after-school centers into miniature schools. Intensive use of after-school hours for strictly academic purposes is not uncommon among middle-class families in Japan and Korea. In that context, the drive for achievement has become an overarching goal for many parents, though critics argue that those children are being deprived of their childhood.[34] In the communities we studied, however, academic accomplishment did not enjoy this kind of inordinate privilege and the schools generated a good deal of negative response. Frankly, given the words of the youth we interviewed and the clear preponderance of research findings on schools for early adolescents, the idea of making these urban youth clubs more like schools does not seem like a very smart move. This is not to suggest that after-school centers should have no academic components. All the clubs had assigned time for homework and several had tutoring programs. However, these components are most successful when integrated into the overall climate of the club, which provides more freedom to adolescents than does school. Indeed, some of the more promising school-based experiments in after-school programming, such as the NYC Beacons, depart dramatically from the business-as-usual school model, basing their program instead on a youth development model.[35] There are examples of youth organizations that have successfully designed programs that are predominantly academically oriented,[36] but launching programs that replicate the typical school experience seems sure to lead to disappointment.

In contrast to school, the club serves as a caring, personal community.[37] The youth there saw it as a home-place where they are able to express themselves. The club serves as a supportive environment in which youth can develop different aspects of their emerging identities and have a number of their developmental needs met. The story of Tiffany, who was quoted briefly earlier, illustrates the club's role in providing this type of support.

TIFFANY: BEING YOURSELF
AND SPEAKING YOUR MIND

Tiffany is a 13-year-old African American girl who has been a regular member at the East Side club for 4 years. She dresses in typical early adolescent fashion, walking the line between kids' and adolescents' clothing styles. Tiffany's attitude shifts easily from being extremely enthusiastic and friendly to being more dismissive and cynical. Her facial expression tends to appear serious or aloof, but once she is engaged in conversation she smiles and laughs. Although she often acts bored or uninterested when approaching a club activity, she gets drawn in once she begins to participate.

When we first came to the club, Tiffany was fairly quiet and appeared to be socially isolated from the other children. She spent time with one or two girls her age but more often she hung out alone and did not socialize with the predominant group of girls her age. Tiffany adores volleyball and played on the club's girls' team our first year at the club. She loved to practice volleyball and spent time just hitting the ball around by herself or with some of the researchers at the club. Although she loved to play, Tiffany never seemed to really interact with the other girls on the team. After 1 year she quit the team, citing conflicts with the older girls. Tiffany never appeared to be completely a part of the social group of girls her age. Despite this, she came to the club daily and was engaged in a wide variety of groups and activities, including sports, leadership activities, and psychoeducational groups.

In our second year at the club, Tiffany began to hang out more with the other girls her age. She talked more frequently with a few of the core group of 14-year-old girls who hung around together and became closer to some of them. These girls were all members of the various girls sports teams and cheerleading squad. She also began to play cards with one or two boys her age. Tiffany clearly made significant strides socially at the club.

The importance of her club relationships is underscored when she compares the club with school. Tiffany reports having more friends, and closer friends, at the club than at school. She says that she hardly talks to anyone at school but at the club she talks to everyone, because she likes the kids at the club better than those at school. Tiffany also says that she joined all of the activities that she does at the club because friends were in them. The other kids at the club are one of the primary reasons that Tiffany gives for why she thinks of the club as a second home:

Because it's a place you have fun and spend time with friends. It's like being with your family and having fun and stuff. Because all the kids get along good and that's how you are with your family.

In addition to her friends at the club, Tiffany reports a close relationship with Cheryl, the female staff person who coaches the volleyball team and leads a number of activities for girls. Tiffany reports that she talks about "everything," including personal things, with Cheryl. Cheryl has taught Tiffany things including "how to take care of myself and not do bad stuff that will make [me] feel bad." In addition, Cheryl has directly helped Tiffany negotiate difficult situations, including stepping into a fight she was having with another girl and convincing the girls to work out their differences without fighting. Tiffany says that Cheryl "makes me feel better after I talk to her. If I feel sad, I talk to her and feel better inside." She particularly likes Cheryl because she feels that Cheryl doesn't act like the typical adult, but "acts like a friend. She's younger so she's gone through the same stuff. If you ask her something she won't say it like she's an adult. She'll say it like she's a friend." Tiffany says that the club would still feel like a home without Cheryl, because of another female staff person who, Tiffany says, is "like a grandma to me." Like most of the other youth we interviewed, Tiffany is responding to what she feels is an overall climate of caring and not just one individual staff member.

When asked where she feels more like herself, at the club or at school, Tiffany says that she feels most like herself at the club. Tiffany's reason for this, which was previously given, bears repeating here:

I express myself more at the club. I speak my mind. I'm not afraid to say what I say. In school you get in trouble. I can say anything here, speak my mind. I'm more myself.

Tiffany goes on to say that she feels best about herself at the club because she expresses herself and says "what I have to say instead of hiding it." Like Sammy, whose statement opened this chapter, Tiffany sees the club as a place to express what she sees as her total self. Through the support of a variety of close relationships and activities at the club, Tiffany feels able to speak her mind. In particular, Tiffany reports that there is more freedom at the club than at school, in terms of both the autonomy to do different activities, have fun, and relax and the freedom to act like herself. The club, therefore, is providing Tiffany, as it did for Sammy, a unique setting to express multiple sides of herself. The ease of activity and expression provided within the walls of the club allows Tiffany to be a kid, to have fun, and to form positive relationships with both peers and adults, all of which support her development.

THE PRESENT AND THE FUTURE

To have a place where one feels at home is something special and worth having, whatever one's age. It has intrinsic value. It brings fullness, comfort, and joy to life. Even if such places played no role in the future, had no impact on development, they would still be important and adults should do what they can to help create such places for youth.

For adolescents growing up in poor urban communities, the youth center as home-place also provides a valuable bridge to the outside world. One of the hardest tasks for social policy has been to find ways in which young people can feel connected to the wider society. Social scientists have referred to this feeling as a sense of social integration.[38] Community-based after-school programs can serve as a setting in which youth connect with broader social institutions and the wider adult community. These organizations are often well regarded and respected institutions within inner cities. Adolescents who come to call the club a home have developed an attachment to a place that is socially approved and linked to other institutions in their communities and beyond. Given the decline of many institutions in the inner city, these connections may be especially important for minority and low-income youth.[39]

Educators have tried for decades, without much success, to create environments specially designed for the needs of early adolescents. Over the course of the 20th century, junior high schools, and then middle schools, were developed as transitional environments, to ease young people from the more comforting climate of elementary school to the more impersonal environment of the high school.[40] The failure of such schools is particularly disadvantageous for inner-city youth, as they have few other opportunities to learn how to successfully navigate organizational life, a crucial skill for a productive adulthood. The type of after-school program that we have studied enables inner-city youth to acquire some of these skills and social capital. At these sites, youth voluntarily conform to norms, rules, and requirements of dress and behavior—and even enforce these rules with each other. Most club members did not experience these rules as restrictive, in contrast to the way they talked about school rules. The clubs thus provide a nonfamilial setting in which societal rules for conduct are learned and integrated into their emerging sense of self.

These centers incorporate some of the best qualities of family and home so that youth become an integral part of a functioning community. They can have fun with friends and caring relationships with adults and prepare for adult life. After-school programs do not have to be designed to do one but not the other.

NOTES

1. Proshansky, Fabian, & Kaminoff (1983); Rubinstein & Parmelee (1992).
2. Moos (1976).
3. Eccles et al. (1993).

4. Branch (1999); Clark (1992); Flannery, Huff, & Manos (1998).

5. Low & Altman (1992).

6. Chawla (1992); Cotterell (1991, 1993); Korpela (1989, 1992); Korpela & Hartig (1996); Low & Altman (1992); Marcus (1992); Rubinstein & Parmelee (1992).

7. Korpela (1989, 1992); Korpela & Hartig (1996).

8. Feldman & Stall (1994); Relph (1976).

9. Werner, Altman, & Oxley (1985).

10. Feldman & Stall (1994); hooks (1990).

11. Rapoport (1985).

12. Eccles et al. (1993); Grotevant (1998); Steinberg (1990).

13. Markus & Nurius (1986); Harter (1990); Harter, Bresnick, Bouchey, & Whitesell (1997).

14. Burton, Allison, & Obeidallah (1995); Harter (1990); Harter et al. (1997); McLaughlin (1993).

15. Harter (1990); Harter et al. (1997); Heath & McLaughlin (1993); McLaughlin (1993).

16. See Hirsch and Jolly (1984) for an extended discussion of how social networks can support multiple roles.

17. Chawla (1992); Cotterell (1993); Korpela & Hartig (1996); Marcus (1992).

18. Pastor, McCormick, and Fine (1996) studied a small group of urban girls. For these authors, the home-place is where girls are able to connect to each other and to their inner selves—a place for exploration and resisting stereotypes that does not exist elsewhere for urban minority girls.

19. To examine the combined effects of demographic variables and site (i.e., membership at one club versus another) on a youth's report of the club as a home, a logistic regression model was developed. Logistic regression is a form of linear regression developed for use with categorical variables. Logistic regression of the independent factors site, race, age group (10–12, 13–14, 15–18), and sex on the 0/1 variable whether or not the youth considers the club as a home revealed a marginally significant main effect for site ($p < .056$). None of the other three factors in the model (sex, age, or race) were significant.

20. A total of 17 responses (21%) received no major code. The subcategories could fall under the umbrella of any of the two major categories with the exception of relationships, which could only be coded under psychosocial. A response that received no major code could still receive one or more subcodes.

21. All codes had satisfactory inter-rater reliability (kappa ranged from .89 to 1.0).

22. Responses that did not specifically mention the other children involved in the activity were not coded for relationships.

23. Responses that referred only to the youth being able to choose what they do at the club, without reference to a specific activity, were *not* coded as activity. Such responses were seen as focusing on the autonomy of the child, rather than

on the activity itself (e.g., "I can do what I want here"). Responses such as "they do what I like to do" *were* coded as activity; however, they were seen as referring to more specific preferred behaviors, even though the particular activity was not named.

24. Franklin (1988); Gutman (1976); Shimkin, Shimkin, & Frate (1978); Staples & Johnson (1993); Sudarkasa (1988).

25. See ethnographic studies by Aschenbrenner (1978); Martin and Martin (1978); Stack (1974, 1996).

26. Hirsch, Mickus, & Boerger (2002); Rhodes, Contreras, & Mangelsdorf (1994); Taylor (1996); Taylor & Roberts (1995); Valenzuela & Dornbusch (1994).

27. Eccles et al. (1993).

28. See Pianta (1999) for an extensive discussion of student relationships with teachers.

29. Warren et al. (2002).

30. Halpern (1999); McLaughlin et al. (1994).

31. Hirsch & Rapkin (1987); Seidman (in press).

32. Lipsitz (1984).

33. Brown (1999).

34. Cho (1995); Field (1995).

35. Pittman et al. (2000); Warren et al. (2002).

36. McLaughlin et al. (1994).

37. Hirsch (1981).

38. James Coleman has written forcefully on this topic (e.g., 1961; President's Science Advisory Committee, 1974).

39. Hirsch, Roffman, Deutsch, Flynn, Loder, & Pagano (2000).

40. See excellent history by Cuban (1992).

4

ONE-STOP SHOPPING
FOR MENTORING

Programs that provide youth with adult mentors are enormously popular. These programs consistently receive positive press and are supported across the political spectrum. The appeal is undeniable, but the reality of making these programs work is another story. The process of matching volunteer adults with willing youths often does not work. Among high-poverty youth, it has been estimated that up to two thirds of mentoring relationships do not survive the introductory phase.[1] One critical reason for these failures to connect is straightforward: The adults and youth are typically from extremely different worlds. For example, a White, college-educated, middle-class, suburban adult has just so much in common with a Black or Latino inner-city youth. Even if they do have some interests in common (such as sports), their contrasting behavioral and linguistic styles can easily prevent them from successfully exploring domains of mutual interest. Unfortunately, youth fare poorly when exposed to relationships that do not last long.[2]

Poor African American communities typically had a natural, home-grown source of adult mentors. Called "old heads" or "othermothers," these men and women lived in the same community as the youth and had a reputation for wisdom, supportiveness, and effectiveness.[3] As inner-city communities deteriorated over the past decades, with the loss of their middle class and businesses and the weakening of many social institutions, so too, it is believed, has many a neighborhood found itself bereft of its wise heads.

Although they may no longer hang out on the front steps of their house, good local mentors can still be found in community-based after-school programs. Early in our time in the clubs, we were struck by the warmth and caring readily evident in the relationships between club staff and youth, and the ways in which these adults strove to educate their charges about the ways of the world.[4]

Charles is one such old head. He is the sports director of the East Side Boys & Girls Club. The club is located near a public housing project and most youth who attend the club live in this project. The apartment buildings are in better condition than much other public housing, but it is still not a very safe place at night. There are three local gangs in the general area. Nearby are railroad yards and single-family houses. It feels isolated, far away from the city center. Helping club youth break out of this isolation is a main concern of Charles and the other staff.

A 30ish Black man of medium build, Charles spends most of his time with guys ages 10 and older, though he is popular with the girls as well. One day, Terrenda White, a young African American woman who was one of our research assistants at the club, interrupted Charles while he was cleaning up a room and got him to talk about the various ways in which he seeks to help the male adolescents at the club. The conversation took place in the fall, during Terrenda's fourth visit to the club, when she was still getting acquainted with the place. As they talked, more and more guys, and a few girls, dropped by to listen in. I am going to present Terrenda's extensive field notes on this conversation, and then use them as a vehicle for discussing the various ways in which Charles, and other staff, mentor these youth. The field notes capture Charles in a storytelling mode with a group of young people. They reflect his favorite mentoring style, which is used by a number of other staff at these sites.

The following field notes pick up the conversation with Charles describing how new programs for girls, led by Cheryl (staff member discussed in previous chapter), inspired him to begin a discussion group with guys. Charles uses not only the vocabulary but also the rhetorical strategies (as will be discussed later) of vernacular African American English to connect and convey his points in a style that is culturally consonant to the youth.

> "When I [Charles] first came here . . . some of the girls be walking around here with low self-esteem and stuff. I be telling them not to worry about what people say. So what, someone call you ugly. They said bad stuff about Jesus Christ, too. So, you know, [Cheryl] doing stuff with them, helped them with they self-esteem and everything. But soon, when [the guys] saw the stuff the girls were doing, they was like, 'why can't we do this? why can't we do that?'" He went on to say that it was during that time that he started his discussion group. One guy . . . looking about 14 years old . . . sat down in a chair next to me and listened to the conversation.

Charles went on, "I would stay up to 'bout 2 in the morning recording stuff [for the group] like Maury Povich and bring it in the next day to talk about issues on the show and have a debate. I even let them watch that movie called Kids so that we could talk about AIDS and stuff. It had cursing in it. They [club leadership] don't really like us to show stuff with cursing in it, but," he paused and looked down at the boy sitting between us, shrugging, and said, "they curse. They all curse. So it was really no big deal. I thought it was a good movie for them to watch.

We talk about sex and everything. See some of these guys didn't even know what a wet dream was! They thought it was when you peed on yourself. They be like, 'yeah, it's when you go to the bathroom on yourself, right,'" he laughed. By this time, two other guys had walked in. . . . I found out later . . . that they were 15 years old. They sat on the other side of me on the couch and were listening to Charles' words as well. Charles joked again about the boys not knowing about wet dreams, and the boys laughed and looked at each other. "See we be thinking they too young to know about all that stuff, but it's better they learn about that stuff here than out there on the streets, you know."

[By this time, I [Terrenda] was seriously trying not to blush. It was somewhat awkward for me being the only girl in the room, literally surrounded [now] by guys. . . . One of the guys near me sitting on the couch was the guy I played basketball with on my last visit. Then, with all of his 'trash talking' while playing, he had attempted, or at least [it seemed] so to me, to appear tough and 'hard.'[5] Now, however, as Charles talked, he was smiling and blushing with his head somewhat bowed. . . .]

He went on to answer my previous question [regarding the age at which he allows youth into his discussion group]. "Any age they want to come. I don't have an age limit. If they want to know, they can come. Even some of the girls last year would come and we would just talk about stuff. . . . Yeah, 'cause at first these girls would be getting pregnant and stuff. They still call they self doing stuff, but nothing really. When we have dances or sleepovers, they be trying to sneak over together or whatnot." The guys began laughing and smiling as Charles looked at them while telling me the information; Charles was laughing as well. "But they know not to try anything, because they know what me and Cheryl expect of them and they respect us just like we respect them."

"But these guys were bad when I first came," Charles added, but not really pointing to anyone in particular. Laughing and shaking his head, he said, "I remember one time this little boy cursed me out. At the time, I didn't really let it show that I was laughing. But he, what did he call me? He called me all kinds of names, like mother-this and all kinds of stuff. And see, I'm from the South, I'm used to 'yes, ma'am' and 'yes, sir.' Naw, that little boy cursed me out! I mean he was like almost a toddler! And they used to have fights like everyday, man, every day somebody was fighting. But they better now, though. Except him," Charles said while pointing to one of the guys on my right. "See, he messing up in school." The boy just looked at Charles with a slight smile on his face. Charles wasn't smiling back, however.

Charles, still not smiling, continued on, "And see I know other people have them [these guys] stereotyped as scavengers or something. When we go over to Hamilton [a park district] to play flag football, the coach be cheating and calling them names and stuff. I almost got in a fistfight with him one time. See, I didn't even want to take them over there to play with them. Every time we go over there, he just be talking all negative about them and stuff, but they keep begging me to go over there. And he be cheating all the time, but I be telling my boys they don't have to take that type of mess from nobody. Why should they? Cause he think, somehow, that 'cause his kids live across the street they somehow better than our boys because they live in the projects.

But I be teaching [the guys] all kinds of stuff. When I first came, all they did was play basketball. I got tired of basketball. I know 'cause they from this big city, basketball was everything. You know, coming from the South, though, football is what I'm into. But even other stuff. Volleyball, they saw the girls playing." At this point, one of the three guys added, "Yeah, they got they own team!" Charles went on, "But see I started teaching them other stuff. They had all kinds of equipment here. They learned golf, badminton, and even hockey. None of them had ever play badminton, but 'bout when we went to the tournament we won half the trophies." One of the other guys added in at this point how cool badminton was.

Charles continued, "With hockey now, we ain't that good, but that's all right. When we went to the tournament, we got our butts whooped! But we didn't even care, our guys were having fun, that's all that mattered to us. And we be inviting other clubs to play with us in the tournaments. I tried to get a basketball tournament going, but people kept complaining that they didn't have transportation here. But them other clubs, like them Spanish clubs and Forest, with some of them White people, they keep giving us excuses. They just don't want to play with us, you know. But that's all right. . . ."

"Cheryl walked in and started joking about the NBA [basketball] player Allen Iverson, who was currently on the television playing in a basketball game. She and Charles joked about getting tickets once to a basketball game just to see him, but that Iverson did not show up because of sickness. They went on about all the good tickets and seats they get to the basketball games as Boys & Girls club staff. "You mean seats right near the court?" I [Terrenda] asked with my voice rising and eyebrows lifted. Charles nodded and informed me that he usually takes some of his guys in the club with him to see the game. "We walked in one time on the floor. . . . This is the only part of the stadium I think that has ushers, too. We walked in and all these, you know, rich White people all dressed up were there and me, looking all dingy with my shorts and T-shirt on. . . . I didn't have time to change 'cause I had just got the tickets at the last minute. Anyway, the usher came up to us and checked our tickets, you know, to make sure we belonged. It was so funny because by the end, the guys were dancing all in the aisles and stuff, and before you know, the White people were dancing with 'em too. We had so much fun, man."

By this time there were about two more guys in the room sitting near us and watching Charles tell me stories about their outings. . . . I remember one guy, who looked about 16, said to another guy who had come in the room, talking *loudly and trying to get Charles' attention, "Be quiet, he talking, man." After commanding the boy to hush, he [the 16-year-old boy] turned his attention back to our conversation. [More guys and girls then entered the room.]*

Cheryl was still in the room and was walking around, fumbling through magazine racks and quickly flipping through magazines as if she were looking for something. She added to the conversation a few times as Charles told me about their experiences at sports games. Charles added that he liked the cheerleading idea for the girls because it got the younger girls involved with the older girls. Cheryl mentioned that the girls recently had a big conference [girls from all the local clubs attended]. Charles replied, looking at me, "See, the guys, we could never have any of the stuff. 'Cause the guys don't know how to act when they with other guys. One group of guys be trying to be harder than the other group. If one guy step on another guy's shoes or something simple like that, then they wanna fight and everything." . . . When more kids came running into the room, they asked Charles when the next game of basketball was going to start. "Y'all wanna play again? I'm tired, man," Charles said, standing up and walking slowly around the chair with his back slightly bent over. He told them that they could play again and began heading toward the door as all the guys got up to go play as well.

Notice how Charles went from reporting on how he mentored, to mentoring. This kind of spontaneity, of grabbing moments to connect and teach as they arise naturally, happens frequently at the clubs. Before discussing the messages that Charles sought to convey, I wish to examine the way in which he communicated.

It is obvious that Charles made considerable use of vernacular African American English. In addition to his words, expressions, and grammar, Charles used rhetorical strategies common to this discourse. Particularly prominent was the way in which he went from topic to topic, but kept returning to some issues. As Geneva Smitherman explained,

> the story-telling tradition is strong in Black American culture. . . . Black English speakers will render their general, abstract observations about life, love, people in the form of a concrete narrative. . . . The relating of events (real or hypothetical) becomes a Black rhetorical strategy to explain a point, to persuade holders of opposing views to one's own point of view, and in general to 'win friends and influence people.' This meandering away from the 'point' takes the listener on episodic journeys and over tributary rhetorical routes, but like the flow of nature's rivers and streams, it all eventually leads back to the source.[6]

She then went on to state that "all of these folk narrative forms have as their overriding theme the coping ability, strength, endurance . . . and power of Black people."[7]

Charles' talk was culturally grounded in its style and in its aims. It encouraged informality and a rapport with his audience. It generated intimacy beyond that provided by some of the topics. It imbued the occasion with added meaning and power. His style of talking is likely part of why the entourage listened with such rapt attention.

In recounting the experiences he had with club youth in and outside of the club, Charles is creating a narrative of shared meaning not only about the club, but also about Black maleness. His function in part resembled that of the griot in traditional African culture. The griot was a revered elder who maintained the history of the group (in the age context of the club, a 30ish adult qualifies as an elder). This history "was not merely the chronicles of who did what when, but composite word-pictures of the culture, belief, ethics, and values of the tribe."[8]

Let us examine the three broad themes or messages that Charles conveyed to the group.

APPRECIATION AND TRUST

"They respect us just like we respect them"

There is little doubt that for Charles, these are *his* kids. He values their talents and abilities and is enthusiastic about them. He respects them as whole, complex persons. He does not view them as problem kids; there is no deficit orientation at work here. The incidents that he recounts with the Hamilton coach provide clear evidence of his commitment to club youth and willingness to stand up and protect them. He is someone they can trust.

This is not a one-way street. There is mutual rapport, understanding, and appreciation. The guys recognize him as someone whose views count and who commands respect (e.g., as witnessed by the shutting up of one guy who was interrupting).

The presence of this level of appreciation and trust is further emphasized when an alternative scenario is imagined. The guys could have reacted with indignation to his sharing such intimate details of their sexual ignorance, especially in the presence of a young woman who, after all, is merely 5 years their elder. They could have felt disrespected and humiliated, and yelled at Charles while storming out of the room. Anyone who knows teenagers knows that this scenario is not implausible, yet it did not take place—indeed, quite the opposite occurred.

Jean Rhodes has suggested that trust is an essential element of mentoring relationships.[9] It is likely that this trust evolved out of many shared activities and situations, which engendered mutual appreciation. These qualities likely provided the conditions for effectively communicating the other two principal messages.

COMFORT WITH SELF

"But that's all right"

When one looks at Charles, it is clear that he is comfortable in his body. He is solid, but relaxed, muscular, but loose. He talks of how he shrugged off the little boy who was cursing at him. He speaks with ease of intimate sexual details, such as wet dreams. The comfort is social as well as physical: He feels little hesitation about using vernacular African American English with a college student whom he met only recently.[10]

I believe that Charles' central concern was with helping his young charges develop a similar sense of comfort with who they are and who they are becoming. Indeed, many psychologists, beginning with Erik Erikson, have considered the development of an identity the overarching developmental task of adolescence.[11] Charles seeks to have them become comfortable with diverse aspects of their developing selves, with their body and body image, with girls, with intimate self-disclosure. He introduces them to new learning experiences and sports, which can provide the basis for elaborated identities. New sports include even a somewhat esoteric activity such as badminton. Much more of a middle- to upper-class activity, with associations with the English aristocracy, badminton could well be considered effeminate by others in this inner-city housing project, but one guy lets us know that it is "cool."

Sometimes learning how to enjoy and be skilled at a variety of activities involves blending qualities that might otherwise appear incompatible. Charles encourages their competitiveness and applauds their success, but also emphasizes that losing is OK as well, that one can still gain pleasure even if one does not win. He helps youth learn that they can be hard sometimes, yet soft at others; this was probably revealed most exquisitely by the teen who talked trash to Terrenda while playing basketball the week before, but sat blushing next to her, with his head bowed, when Charles talked about wet dreams.

An important part of identity development in adolescence is imagining a possible place for oneself in the larger, adult world.[12] The reception these youngsters receive at Hamilton is an indication of the obstacles they confront coming from the projects, even among other low-income groups. However, Charles does what he can to help them negotiate this turf. He also brings and introduces them to the world of White folk. In procuring high-priced professional basketball tickets, he very concretely places them among even well-to-do Whites. They understand that they are not automatically given entrance, even at a game, to such a world (the ushers checked "to make sure we belonged"). However, the happy ending to their time at the game suggests that with proper credentials they can find an acceptable place without sacrificing who they are in the process ("by the end, the guys were dancing in the aisles and stuff, and before you know, the White people were dancing with 'em too").

Charles recognizes that being comfortable with one's developing self is not without its stresses and strains. His repeated refrain, "but that's all right," tries to buffer them against that stress. If they do not automatically take things as a threat, they are less likely to become aroused and stressed and perhaps wind up doing things that get them in trouble, perhaps serious trouble. The refrain, and the comforting way in which Charles spoke it, is a way to help them develop skills in what Heinz Kohut would call self-soothing:[13] learning skills in emotional self-regulation, an essential component of learning to adapt successfully.

Above all, Charles is mentoring their development into men. He helps them assemble the various parts (e.g., sports, sexuality, academics) and put them together. He helps them deal with the dualities that are part of the construction of gender identity (e.g., hard/soft). These are difficult tasks for young teenage guys wherever they may be, but special challenges are faced by those growing up in poor, urban communities, and most especially those living in government-funded housing projects.[14] They have to face long-standing stereotypes about being hypersexualized and violent predators (witness the Hamilton coach who called them scavengers).[15] Whether they will find an acceptable place in the outside world is more than a passing adolescent daydream: Unemployment or jail is a real possibility and many realistically fear that they will not live long enough to reach their 30s.[16] So Charles' mentoring takes on a distinct urgency and salience. Indeed, it is the seriousness of the challenges that are faced that likely led Charles to the third theme of his remarks.

BEHAVIOR EXPECTATIONS

"Then they wanna fight and everything"

Charles is concerned not only with how these youth can develop important understandings, skills, and behaviors, but also with preventing them from getting into trouble. There are lots of ways a young fellow from the projects can get into trouble, and Charles is picky about what is worth spending his social capital on. Cursing, clearly, is not high on his priority list. He pays only limited, though pointed, attention to education on this particular occasion, though he has been known to keep youth out of the gym if they are failing in school. What does concern him, the theme to which he returns more than once, is fighting and violence.

The nature of violence in these communities has changed since the advent of crack cocaine in the 1980s.[17] Previously, fighting was done with fists (at times with knives). Now, guns are common, so instead of a bloody nose, confrontations can and sometimes do lead to sudden death. Charles realizes that bad things will happen that will make them want to respond. He, himself, felt like punching the Hamilton coach, showing the guys that his instincts are not unlike theirs (and perhaps in the process increasing his credibility as a role model to them). However, he resisted. Violent incidents often start with simple matters that get out of hand, and with access to guns, things can turn deadly quickly.[18] So Charles cautions them to not respond to provocations (e.g., someone stepping on someone else's foot). He praises them for their progress in this area and suggests possible rewards (e.g., a conference, like the girls had, where they can get together with youth from other clubs) if they do better still.

A WIDE RANGE OF MENTORING

If there is anything clear about Charles, it is that he engages in a lot of mentoring about a wide variety of issues. Charles is far from alone in that work. Indeed, it is one of the distinguishing marks of the clubs in general. Moreover, this mentoring is done with a variety of techniques and in varied relational and environmental settings.

The range of life domains that Charles addresses with the guys is impressive. He deals with the most intimate details of puberty in highly personal terms. Yet he is not alone in this. I could instead have talked in detail of how important it was to a group of 12-year-old Hispanic girls to be able to talk about their periods with Aurelia, a female staff member. And what it meant to the girls that Aurelia was unprepared for the onset of one of her own periods during a trip with the girls, and her willingness to discuss this openly with them. Various staff members discuss other matters of sexuality, such as birth control and sexually transmitted diseases. Sometimes sexuality comes up in regard to others; for example, Aurelia counseled some girls about how to handle things when a mother brought a man over and the girls heard loud noises coming from the mother's bedroom. However, not everything that Charles or Aurelia discusses is so intimate. Almost all staff members are involved to some extent with the academic life of club youth. They encourage their vocational aspirations and give advice on how to make one's way in a work organization. As has been seen with both Cheryl (in the previous chapter) and Charles, they deal with issues that come up with friendships and peer interactions. They spend considerable time teaching skills in sports and coaching sports games—something of considerable salience to the girls as well as the boys. Granted, not all staff mentored as widely as did Charles. However, in considering what we observed across these six sites, it is difficult for me to think of a single domain of life that one should address with an adolescent that was not addressed at some point by staff in these organizations. Indeed, what we observed across sites suggests the range of mentoring that could be provided at every site.

Not only do staff mentor youth around a wide range of life domains, but they do so in numerous ways. When Tiffany continued to get along poorly with other girls, Cheryl helped by guiding Tiffany in developing new interpersonal skills and understandings, by providing emotional support to keep her on track, and by actively mediating between the girls during some conflicts. In addition to serving as a role model, Charles directly taught new sports and used the more indirect teaching strategies of vernacular African American English discourse. Some staff used their personal funds to pay college application fees for youth who could not afford them. Other staff served as advocates for youth when they got in trouble at school or accompanied them to sensitive medical appointments. Although not all staff used all these approaches, the ways of mentoring were many.

The settings in which staff mentored youth were also varied. Some mentoring took place one-on-one. Other times it took place in group contexts. Some groups were one gender only, other times they were mixed; some groups had youth mostly of one age, at other times the group consisted of children of widely different ages. Some groups were fairly small, others larger. Staff sometimes worked together with parents and with teachers. And not all mentoring occurred within the club itself. There were field trips to other clubs, schools, museums, and college campuses.

Results from our quantitative assessment are consistent with our ethnographic findings. We asked our main interview sample of 112 youth from the four clubs we studied during Year 1 to respond to a series of questions concerning mentoring provided by their closest staff contact. The responses were rated by youth on a 1–5 frequency scale. For each item, a majority of youth indicated that their club mentor either always or often provided that quality. Thus, 70% of youth reported that this staff person either always or often gave useful advice for dealing with problems, 69% reported that the staff person pushed them to succeed, 57% were introduced to new ideas, 57% learned how to do things from watching the staff person, and 54% indicated that the staff person had qualities that the youth would like to have (again, all percentages refer to responses of either *always* or *often*). There were no statistically significant differences between clubs on these variables.[19]

YOUTH–ADULT RELATIONSHIPS
IN FORMAL MENTORING PROGRAMS

I have presented a variety of data to suggest the strength of mentoring relationships between adult staff and youth at these clubs. The characteristics of these relationships are placed in greater relief when compared with findings from research on mentoring relationships in other types of programs. Some of these programs have been in existence for quite some time, such as Big Brothers, Big Sisters, though most are of recent vintage: Nearly half of all active mentoring programs in the United States were established between 1994 and 1999, and only 18% have been operating for more than 15 years.[20] Although enthusiasm for such programs is widespread and growing, objective evaluations of their impact have consistently offered a more critical perspective.[21] On the basis of a recent meta-analysis of 55 evaluations, David DuBois and colleagues concluded that mentoring programs were associated with positive gains in education and mental health, but that on average the effect sizes were disappointing, even for established programs such as Big Brothers Big Sisters.[22] Several characteristics of more effective mentoring relationships and programs were identified in this review, as well as in other recent empirical work. It will be instructive to examine whether relationships at after-school programs such as these clubs match the profile of effective relationships found in formal mentoring programs.

Among the characteristics identified by DuBois and colleagues were that effective programs were more likely to be community- rather than school-based, and to target youth at some environmental disadvantage, such as poverty. It is clear that the clubs are community based and, with 86% of our main interview sample receiving subsidized school lunch, have a high-poverty population.

With regard to the nature of the relationships themselves, the amount of contact between mentors and mentees is important. Frequent, regular contact in relationships that last 1 year or more results in larger gains.[23] Data from our main interview sample indicate that youth spend substantial amounts of time with the adult staff member to whom they are closest: 76% get together 4 to 5 days a week, with another 19% getting together 2 to 3 days a week. Thus, frequency of contact is considerably greater than is characteristic of ties in formal mentoring programs and suggests that strong relationships may develop much more quickly at these types of after-school programs. This is important, given that the clubs have a high staff turnover rate, which is true of youth development organizations worldwide.[24] The almost daily interaction affords staff a variety of additional benefits. They are able to observe youth across varied moods and situations, gaining a greater knowledge of them; this knowledge, moreover, does not depend entirely on what the teen chooses to tell them. The frequent contact also provides the opportunity to respond to youth concerns as they arise naturally. Staff are able to address whatever is on a young person's mind that day, enabling their interactions to have an immediacy that can facilitate mentoring effectiveness.

The final set of variables identified by DuBois and colleagues focuses on interactional and experiential characteristics of the relationship. Relationships that provide emotional closeness and support, as well as instrumental assistance, are related to the length of the mentoring relationship and the potential of the mentor to make positive changes in the lives of youth.[25] Furthermore, relationships that involve the youth in decision making and in which the pair engage in friendship-like activities (e.g., hanging out, going to events together, playing sports, having fun) appear especially beneficial.[26] To be effective, mentors apparently should function as friends or companions as well as guides or teachers.[27]

Club staff are quite oriented toward developing multifaceted relationships with youth. Staff frequently respond to youth initiative in deciding on activities (e.g., Charles taking them to the Hamilton park district gym against his own personal wishes).[28] All staff spend time with youth engaging in recreational or companionship-type activities. And certainly staff such as Charles provide substantial amounts of emotional and instrumental support. In rating the closeness of their relationship with their primary staff contact, 68% of youth in our main interview sample rated their relationship as either 4 or 5 on a 5-point closeness scale (5 = extremely close); only 4% indicated that they were not close (rating = 1).

The multifaceted involvement of staff with club youth extends beyond their dyadic relationship. Most staff have developed ties to important members of the youth's social network: 61% of youth indicated that this staff person knew their family and 88% indicated that the staff person knew their friends. The inclusion of the staff person in the youth's broader social network can deepen the bond between youth and staff, as well as providing staff with additional sources of information about the youth. DuBois and colleagues found that programs that created links between the youth's mentor and parent yielded stronger effects. As will be seen later in the chapter, these network linkages also enable staff to intervene directly in the youth's social network.

The emphasis on friendship and companionship in successful mentee–mentor relationships suggests that these adults have built a relationship in which a focus on youth deficits is not the defining dynamic. As was discussed in the chapter on peer ties, youth need a place where they can be the competent ones, the experts. An emphasis on friendship, companionship, and recreation provides youth with opportunities to express and be recognized for what they enjoy and can do well. Given such appreciation and validation, young people may be more open to the mentor's guidance in other areas, consistent with a reciprocal relationship in which the adolescent does not always have to be one-down. Youth are more likely to be resistant if they are always seen as lacking.

Relationships between adults and youth at this type of comprehensive after-school center may not be officially labeled a "mentoring program," but they match the profile of successful mentoring ties exceptionally well.[29] Indeed, in many ways they go considerably beyond the benchmarks identified in the literature. The adults are around youth, and available to them, for hours at a time almost daily. The relationship develops out of mutual interests, typically of a social or recreational nature, rather than being force-fed from the start. The staff member's involvement extends to other members of the youth's social network. Thus, the benefits of youth–staff relationships at these types of after-school programs may well be greater than in the typical, stand-alone mentoring program.

Our finding on the importance of broad mentoring relationships in after-school programs is consistent as well with a substantial body of developmental research on successful parent–child relationships. A large number of studies have documented the value of what is termed authoritative parenting. This parenting style involves being both highly responsive (warm and validating) and highly demanding (set high standards, monitor behavior, set limits).[30] This approach to interacting with youth is characteristic of the best mentors at the after-school programs we studied.[31]

The range of mentoring at this type of after-school program appears striking. Yet there is an additional comparison that can be made to test even more fully the possible value of these relationships. This involves comparing the club relationship with other important relationships with nonparental adults. Do close kin, for instance, engage in similarly broad mentoring? Additional evidence of the value of these after-school ties will be obtained if those relationships are found to play a distinct role in the lives of these young people. We now turn to those analyses.

COMPARISON WITH CLOSE KIN AND SCHOOL ADULTS

Types of Monitoring

Qualitative data from our main interview sample of 112 youth allowed us to consider the range of mentoring experiences across key relationships in their lives. Each youth was asked to identify the extended family member (adult), club staff, and adult at their school to whom they were closest. We then asked why they liked that person, what they did together or talked about, and why that person was important to them. As part of her dissertation, Jennifer Roffman coded the open-ended responses.[32] We focus here on those responses that included a reference to mentoring activities; to facilitate this, I recoded the mentoring responses into subcategories that address the range of mentoring experiences that are the concern of this book.[33]

Of those school adults coded for mentoring, the overwhelming majority (89%) focused on academic issues. Teachers helped them understand course material and develop an interest in it, and were sometimes noted for encouraging their aspirations for the future:

> She helps me learn. She is never too busy if I ask her to explain something to me. She also believes I can go to college.
>
> He is kind and I have learned a lot from him. He is important because I used to hate English and he has made me more interested in it and I guess I kind of like it now.

Hardly any school adults were reported to mentor about nonacademic concerns (a response could be coded for more than one category). The ratio of academic to nonacademic responses was 5:1.

By contrast, extended-family adults who were coded for mentoring were involved mostly with nonacademic issues.

> I see my aunt almost every day so she knows me really well. She got pregnant when she was my age, so she is always telling me what not to do. She is fun and we have a good time when we are together.
>
> He's fun for an old person, takes you to a lot of places and when you ask a question, he answers the question and also takes it to different points, so you learn more.

Only 16% of kin coded for academic-related mentoring. Compared with teachers, kin had the exact opposite proportion of academic to nonacademic responses, 1:5.

Club staff mixed academic and nonacademic mentoring more than did either school or kin adults. Their ratio of academic to nonacademic responses was 1:2. Thus, like kin, most of their mentoring was around nonacademic issues, but they were reported as mentoring around academic issues (37%) more than twice as often. Indeed, club staff were the only adults of these three who were reported to provide regular help with homework. Nearly half of the nonacademic mentoring revolved around sports.

There were also differences in how kin and club staff provided nonacademic mentoring. Kin were divided evenly between those who emphasized avoiding negative behaviors ("talk about never falling into a gang. [He's] important because he teaches me not to do wrong things") and those who mentored around diffuse issues with a more positive orientation ("shows me how to go through life without always putting yourself down. If someone's talking about you, just get over it and it won't hurt. Use positive side instead of negative fighting"). Avoiding negative behaviors and emphasizing positive, diffuse mentoring were each coded for 26% of kin responses.

Consistent with the emphasis in youth development organizations of promoting positive growth,[34] club staff preferred to engage in diffuse, positive mentoring:

> She is important to me because she is someone I would like to be like. She is there for me when I need to talk and never yells or says that I am no good. She's been through a lot so I know her advice is good. I come here because I know she cares.
>
> He's like a friend to me. He acts like a grown-up, too, but has a good way with kids. He likes helping people. If you're a basketball player, he'll help you with what you need. [We] mainly talk about sports and life and going to college.

In contrast to kin, club staff were more likely to have diffuse, positive mentoring relationships (30%) than to focus on avoiding negative behaviors

(15%). It is possible that this kin versus club staff difference may reflect different issues discussed with youth. For example, perhaps club staff were more likely to discuss issues that were suitable for diffuse, positive mentoring. We did not have a large enough sample to examine this.

Consistent with our ethnographic data, findings from this phase of our research indicate that club staff provide a wide range of mentoring. Furthermore, they indicate that club staff balance academic and nonacademic mentoring more than either kin or school adults do. Among the closest nonparental adults in the lives of these urban youth, the results suggest that the club staff person engages in the widest range of mentoring along these two critical dimensions.[35]

Mentors and Violence

We next investigated whether club staff, kin, and school adults differ in their ability to buffer these young people from the psychological effects of living in violent neighborhoods. There has been a surge of violence among young Americans which, though apparently having peaked in 1993, remains unusually high.[36] Homicide is the second leading cause of death for 10- to 19-year-olds.[37] Youth living in urban or low-income areas are exposed to the highest levels of community violence.[38] It is not without reason that some investigators have thought of poor urban neighborhoods as "war zones."[39] And within the club setting itself, violence prevention was a major focus for staff such as Charles.

This phase of our research emphasized quantitative analyses with our main interview sample. Statistical analyses of the quantitative data address a glaring gap in the research literature. Youth–staff relationships are widely considered to be an important element of after-school programs and youth development organizations more generally. Nevertheless, studies in which these relationships are assessed at all are sparse.[40] Research reports that include statistical analyses of relationship data are, to the best of my knowledge, nonexistent. In the absence of quantitative data, many social scientists and policymakers are unlikely to be convinced of the value of these ties.

As part of her dissertation research, Maria Pagano set up equations (technically referred to as regression equations) to determine whether the three relationships differed in their ability to influence youth self-esteem depending on the level of neighborhood safety as perceived by the child. Pagano first controlled for a variety of socioeconomic, psychological, and program variables that could influence the results.[41] She also distinguished between positive and negative interactions between youth and the three adults, to make sure that our results reflected positive social support received, rather than a mixture of positive and negative interactions.[42]

The results indicated that greater support from club staff is associated with higher levels of self-esteem for youth in all neighborhoods. However, the association is stronger—matters more—for youth who live in more violent neighborhoods. By contrast, the association between kin or school support and self-esteem did not vary by level of perceived neighborhood safety. Because of the special potency of club support for youth in the most violent neighborhoods, the effect size for the club relationship on self-esteem is twice the size of the effect for closest adult kin and more than four times the size of the effect for the closest tie to a school adult.[43]

After Pagano completed the statistical analyses, I initiated a series of follow-up interviews with youth at the East Side Club to help make sense of these results. These young people had no difficulty in telling us of fistfights they had witnessed or shootings that they had heard or seen in their neighborhood. Often the precipitants of these violent episodes were everyday interactions—gossip, insults—that had spiraled out of control.[44] Sometimes the violence was gang related, and most clubs were near the territory of several gangs.

Although violence can erupt anywhere, the club, kin, and school adults differ in their access to this violence and thus in their ability to intervene. Kin probably have the least access, as very little peer-related violence involving their grandchild or nephew/niece is likely to occur right in front of their residence. Violence, and the threat of violence, does occur in schools, but schools are very large places. Given school size, when there is a violent or potentially violent episode it is likely that the youth's closest adult school tie will be on another floor or the other side of the building, precluding the possibility of his or her intervening and controlling the episode. Moreover, when we considered who might intervene in school violence, the young folk we talked to tended to mention on-site security guards or police officers, rather than the teachers or counselors who were named as their closest school tie. By contrast, staff at these after-school sites are much more likely to be close to any action. The youth who name that staff as their closest tie tend to hang out near that person. And even the largest clubs have significantly less space than do the smallest schools, so that staff can be summoned and arrive quickly at any trouble spot. Accordingly, club staff have greater opportunities to intervene in youth violence. They are also seen as highly effective in doing so, as being very street savvy. We were repeatedly told that "staff here can take care of it," that they "know what to do if something happens," and that if something starts, staff will "break it up."[45]

Marcia Chaiken gives a good account of how staff deal with potentially violent incidents at community-based after-school programs:

> . . . adolescents are very sensitive to challenges from other teenagers made, for example, during a basketball game. Given the frequent violent outcomes on the surrounding streets in similar situations, the adolescents nearby become tense, and telltale "noise" begins. Staff alert to the needs and values of the teenagers immediately break the tension with a simple take-charge action (e.g., blowing a whistle, giving a time-out

sign, or simply walking over to the locus of the challenge), focus the teens on the clear-cut rules, talk quietly to the participants involved in the challenge. . . . No one is blamed, everyone "saves face," and respect is maintained.[46]

Staff at the sites we studied made use of additional actions to intervene in these situations. They would take youth aside to talk through the conflict (sometimes after a brief calming-down period), bring parents in to help resolve conflicts, suspend transgressors, physically restrain combatants, and so on. Chaiken tied such actions to "saving face" and "respect," which begins to provide a link to self-esteem, but more interpretive work needs to be done.

Several decades ago, Abraham Maslow argued that the conflict between the need for safety and growth was imbedded deep in the human psyche.[47] These comprehensive after-school programs provide a site for exploring multiple social identities. This elaboration of self can come to a crashing halt when violence threatens. One youth does not give the other appropriate recognition; indeed, the youth treats the other in a manner that communicates a brutally low opinion of him or her. Preservation rather than elaboration of self now takes precedence.[48] The confrontation dehumanizes, negates hard-won enhancements to self, and strips the youth to a one-dimensional stereotype, posturing—whether boy or girl—with exaggerated macho behavior. The richly articulated self is quickly deflated. Youth who report being in the least safe neighborhoods are probably most sensitive to these threats to their self-esteem.

When staff prevent problematic situations from getting out of hand and quickly return things to normal, their actions prevent the decline in youth self-esteem that can otherwise occur. They validate that the youth is worth protecting, merits respect, and does not deserve to have the self reduced. The richer, elaborated self is protected, with the staff providing the safety net. As one 13-year-old boy told us about the staff person to whom he was closest, "I feel safe when I am with him and I know he will help me out if I need him."

At the same time, staff failure to protect youth on these occasions can negatively impact the youth's self-esteem. Just when the staff person is most needed, just when the youth is particularly vulnerable, that adult fails to come through. Not only does this lead to a temporary diminishment of self, but it likely calls into question the youth's overall relationship with that staff person. The youth may well come to doubt the strength or sincerity of staff support offered at other times. Such an incident may also remind the youth of other occasions when adults failed him or her, which leads to a more generalized loss of self-regard. It is important that the after-school program be a site that is not contaminated by the violence that envelops much of the rest of the youth's world. It needs to be an arena of safety, a place that facilitates and protects development.[49]

How adults respond to instances of actual or potential violence can have a major positive *or* negative impact on youth self-esteem. Young people who live in neighborhoods that they experience as highly unsafe are likely to be most sensitive to threats to their self-esteem arising from violent confrontations and thus most impacted by the effectiveness of adult support. After-school staff are likely to have a greater impact on this process than are kin or school adults because of their greater proximity to violent episodes, which provides them with more opportunities for intervention, as well as greater perceived ability to intervene effectively. Nevertheless, it is important to note that our analyses, based on data reported at a single point in time, do not provide proof of a causal connection between support and self-esteem; longitudinal research, analyzing trends over time, is necessary to clarify the direction of causal influence.[50]

I have now discussed a variety of data on the range and potential value of mentoring relationships at these sites, and compared these both with consensus results from the formal mentoring literature and with relationships developed with key nonclub adults. All of these analyses suggest that staff mentoring relationships are unusually wide ranging. At this point, it is important to provide a theoretical framework for analyzing what these relationships do offer—and could offer.

For those most concerned with practice, the proposed framework can be considered as a type of checklist for assessing staff mentoring efforts. Ideally, staff should be engaged with youth at each level. The greater the range of staff mentoring across these domains, the greater the likely effect.

MENTORING AND
THE CONSTRUCTION OF SELF

The overarching developmental task of adolescence is the construction of an identity, a sense of self, of who one is in the world. The identity-building tasks of youth in low-income urban neighborhoods are especially formidable given poor schools, an absence of jobs, discrimination, and a host of other factors associated with poverty.[51] These young people thus lack certain resources and opportunities for the articulation of self that are available to their age peers in other social classes. Yet many are able to make important strides, regardless, and we need to consider how staff mentors can aid this process.

Identity is a useful orienting objective because its underpinnings pertain to factors in both the person and environment. Adolescents need to construct identities that are personally satisfying as well as viable in some significant component of society.[52] They need to value and feel a sense of oneness with this identity and self,[53] and at the same time find a meaningful home for this emerging self in society. There are numerous difficulties in achieving satisfactory identities in any one sphere of life. Additional problems arise because adolescents, like adults, develop multiple identities or selves, which may not all be in harmony with each other. Some identities or selves that are acceptable in one segment of society (e.g., peers) may be unacceptable in others (e.g., school or work). Before considering these multiple-identity issues, I want to analyze how mentors can help generally in the identity development process.

A sense of initiative is an important building block for identity construction, and it is crucial to have mentors who *foster initiative*. As we observed staff interact with youth in the clubs, we frequently observed the enthusiasm with which staff would respond to youth. A 13-year-old would come up and describe an idea for a new activity, something she had accomplished with her friends, a cool Web site she had found, or money she had raised for a club activity. Charles might tell her how well she had done, whereas Cheryl might beam at her with a big smile. We saw this time and time again, at all of the clubs. This type of interaction plays an important role in Heinz Kohut's psychoanalytic theory of the self. In Kohut's formulation, the "gleam in the mother's eye" mirrors and reinforces what he refers to clinically as the child's grandiosity and exhibitionism. Kohut, however, clearly meant his account to apply as a general description of development, not merely to therapy populations, and saw all people as needing significant others who mirror them throughout life.[54] Translating this into nonclinical terms, we might call this process one of positive responsiveness to the child's expressiveness and ambition. This responsiveness reinforces the capacity for enthusiasm, which lies at the center of a cohesive self.[55] Enthusiasm is vital for fostering initiative, for enabling youth to take the risks that are necessary to achieve, find intimacy, and be creative. In this manner, mentors who respond positively to youth self-expressiveness and ambition can foster their initiative, fueling youth identity development.[56]

Mentors can play a critical role in *socializing youth to particular identities*. They can provide information, guidance, and instruction that are part of the problem-solving process. This information can be given explicitly, implicitly (as Charles did in his conversation), or via observational learning or modeling.[57] They can also provide sanctions that deter youth from pursuing devalued identities, so that wearing gang symbols, for instance, would lead to expulsion from the club. Indeed, for Robert Halpern and colleagues, the main choice that these youth make is whether or not their identity will center around gang membership; participation in youth development sites provides them with a "moratorium" during which they can actively consider a nongang future.[58]

Staff in after-school programs *provide opportunities for skill development*, so that one learns the tools for being successful in a particular activity. Many club youth, for example, participate in fund-raising events to support particular club activities. They learn how to bake cookies, make a sale, account for cash, and so on. This training in business skills and entrepreneurship is not as widely available to youth in impoverished communities through legitimate rather than illegal activities (e.g., selling drugs).

As youths engage in identity-building activities, they can *receive helpful feedback* from mentors. Some of this feedback can be in the form of guided participation, through which mentors give timely guidance or constructive criticism on how to do things well.[59] Feedback can also be given on successful completion of an activity. This kind of feedback can validate the emerging self. Validating feedback from others is considered a critical element of self-development for theorists in the symbolic interactionist tradition.[60] It also promotes personal accomplishment, which provides a sustainable basis for a positive self-concept and place in society.

Emotional support from mentors can also play a vital role.[61] Everyone experiences moments of disappointment and disillusion. Through empathy and encouragement, mentors can keep the adaptive efforts of youth from being derailed. Moreover, mentors can also help youth develop skills in self-soothing, or emotional self-control, that can be drawn on in the future without the mentor's presence.

This formulation, although important, does not as yet consider the troublesome fact that particular identities can be valued in one segment of society, but devalued in others. This critical aspect of identity construction must be addressed, not only in theory, but also in practice, to help youth learn to navigate in often unforgiving environments.

Multiple Identities

When one is growing up, doing well and constructing a satisfactory identity in any one sphere of life can be challenging. The challenges are compounded by the number of life domains in which identities need to be constructed. As one adds identities, a number of systems-level issues arise—issues that can be the hardest of all to resolve.

Codeswitching

Learning what it takes to be accepted among peers in a high-poverty neighborhood is tough enough. It can seem unreal that what has been painfully learned may not do much good—and can even make things worse—in other settings. One very basic domain is the use of language. Vernacular African American English, accepted in the street, is typically disparaged in settings such as schools and places of employment. Youth who wish to succeed in these mainstream arenas must learn what is referred to as standard English. The ability to alternate or mix languages or language varieties is referred to as codeswitching. However, much more than vocabulary and grammar comes into play.[62] Taking a sociolinguistic approach, James Gee argued that to be accepted in other settings, it is necessary to become fluent in the discourse of those worlds:

> Discourses are ways of being in the world, or forms of life which integrate words, acts, values, beliefs, attitudes, and social identities, as well as gestures, glances, body positions, and clothes. A Discourse is a sort of identity kit which comes complete with the appropriate costume and instructions on how to act, talk, and often write, so as to take on a particular social role that others will recognize.[63]

It is not only that youth must learn new discourses; the discourses of mainstream society are often in conflict with those of low-income, minority communities. As Gee noted, "the conflict is between *who* I am summoned to be in this new Discourse . . . and *who* I am in other Discourses that overtly conflict with—and sometimes have historically contested with—this Discourse."[64] Successful codeswitching, therefore, involves not only learning additional discourses, but also learning how to reconcile them when they are inconsistent or in opposition.

These after-school programs provide a bridge between the neighborhood and the mainstream world. Youth can speak vernacular African American English without penalty or reproach. Expressiveness and individuality are appreciated. Communal bonds are encouraged. Hip-hop clothes are OK. However, formal rules exclude certain forms of dress, speech, and behavior, and youth understand that staff (i.e., actual or potential mentors) not only enforce the rules, but believe in them. No gang insignia are permitted. Hats are taken off on entry; excessive jewelry or extremely revealing clothes also are not to be worn. Cursing is not permitted around adults.[65] Physical violence is unacceptable. Staff directives are to be followed. These are the kinds of norms that young people will encounter in mainstream settings.

Staff also mentor youth as to the discourse expected in outside settings. Charles, for example, makes it clear that different clothes are expected and should generally be worn when going to the professional basketball arena ("I didn't have time to change 'cause I had just got the tickets at the last minute"). He also suggests that the guys should restrain their expressive behavior initially until they are accepted in that setting ("by the end, the guys were dancing all in the aisles and stuff"). Charles is far from the only staff member who mentors youth on different discourses. Some of this mentoring is quite explicit. For instance, we witnessed occasions in which other staff have given specific directions on clothes to be worn and acceptable table manners in anticipation of a sponsored dinner at a hotel.

Because codeswitching for these youth will mean, at times, alternating between discordant discourses, two threats to their efforts arise. One of these is internal (the false self), the other external (peer social networks). Mentors at these type of sites can help youth address both of these concerns.

Personal Integrity and the False Self

Acting one way in one setting, and acting very differently somewhere else, is not something that always sits well. Am I being phony by acting so differently? Don't I have enough pride and self-respect to be myself, regardless of who I'm with? Who am I, really? These are issues that can trouble adults, too. However, concerns with phoniness, with inauthenticity, with what Susan Harter refers to as the *false self*, are especially salient to adolescents.[66] It is at that stage of life that one is in the midst of constructing a self, that self-consciousness and uncertainty can run amok, that there is a special vulnerability to feeling false. Youth seem less likely to codeswitch if doing so suggests that they are sacrificing their personal integrity.

Mentors can play a very important role in addressing this concern. It is probably most important for mentors to model their own appreciation of different discourses and comfort in codeswitching among them.[67] Charles, for example, has shown himself to be comfortable with a wide variety of outfits; we have seen him in gym clothes, at other times in more hip attire, and on still other occasions he dresses like a typical guy with an office job. He can speak standard English as well as vernacular African American English. He can be hard and he can be soft. He is respected by Black folk and accepted by White folk. He is all of those things at one time or other; the youth see that and, most important, they see that he is comfortable with all those ways of being. Teenagers are hyperalert to discrepancies between word and deed and cry "hypocrisy" when they see it (or believe they see it). So mentors need to model their comfort in different discourses, in being able to walk the walk as well as talk the talk.

Comfort in different discourses reminds us that the criteria for judging role performance are often ambiguous. What does it take to be a man, and to be recognized as such by others one respects? How does one act in ways that are accepted in the neighborhood as well as mainstream society? Teenagers need these and similar, extremely challenging questions to be addressed concretely, in living reality. Being able to conceptualize the issue in the abstract may have its benefits, but there is no substitute for seeing the lived reality. I suspect it is the same for most adults. There is something invaluable about observing someone who appears to be handling multiple important roles well. Charles, and mentors like him in these types of urban after-school programs, may not be able to explicate fully what it all means, but what they can do is offer themselves as modest examples, and that is really quite a bit.

Social Networks

An individual's social network, which refers to important relationships with family, friends, and others, can have a critical impact on one's identities. Indeed, such a perspective has long been central to the symbolic interactionist approach to understanding identity.[68] Network members can provide or deny resources important to identity development, and they can support or reject efforts to affirm a particular place in the world.

Practitioners who work with youth have long known that networks can sabotage important milestones.[69] Family or friends can overtly reject a youth's effort to do well in school or avoid another pregnancy. Or a girl may fear that success will endanger that support, because she is afraid that by succeeding she may inadvertently be sending a message that she is better than others. Most people need social support for taking bold new steps. Such support is especially important in low-income communities, where there are strong norms of network solidarity and where nonnetwork supports are much fewer but risks are much greater.[70]

A number of social scientists, working in diverse parts of the country, have noted how peer networks have hindered the ability of low-income minority youth to codeswitch. In a study of California minority youth making the transition to a high school in a wealthier neighborhood, Patricia Phelan and colleagues found that few youth were able to develop a peer network for supporting academic success.[71] Some youth were in peer groups that opposed norms for achievement, and doing well in school would have threatened the viability of those friendships. Other youth cut themselves off from neighborhood friends not oriented to academics, but often had considerable difficulty in establishing new friendships with like-minded peers, especially those from different ethnic or social class backgrounds. The transition appeared to be easiest for minority youth who were able to cultivate ties with other academically oriented minority youth.

Katherine Newman found a comparable situation among Harlem (New York City) youth from diverse minority backgrounds who worked at fast-food establishments. Newman found that youth

> who accept low-wage jobs in the fast-food industry must run a gauntlet
> of criticism on the street that is basically relentless. They are taunted,
> shamed, and made to feel that they have capitulated to a social order
> that somehow they should resist.[72]

Many took jobs in other neighborhoods and endured a long commute just to minimize the likelihood that their friends would learn that they were working at fast-food jobs. As they entered early adulthood, these workers increasingly began to socialize more with coworkers and less with neighborhood peers. Like the students in the study by Phelan and colleagues, they needed to create a new peer support network.

Can mentors aid youth in developing supportive peer networks? The California teachers in the Phelan et al. study were reported to be clueless as to the social difficulties their students faced. Even when alert to the issues, it is rare for adults to have the opportunity to intervene directly into youth's social networks. The situation is quite different in the kinds of urban after-school programs that we studied. Youth spend many hours at the site with their friends. Adult staff in these programs get to know and develop relationships with the members of the group, often in a variety of contexts. The adults are used to dealing with youth in a group setting; the youth–staff relationship exists as much within a group as in a dyadic context (in contrast to relationships in programs as Big Brothers Big Sisters, which are typically limited to dyadic, one-on-one interactions). The adults are familiar with the issues within particular peer groups. Adult staff thus have unique opportunities and abilities to intervene directly in youth peer networks.

Because many of their interactions occur in a group context, the messages that adult staff communicate are directed as much at the group as at any individual. Thus, when Charles pointedly castigated one of the guys for not doing well in school, he was doing more than talking to that one fellow. His message was sent to that person's friends as well. They heard it. They knew it applied to them as well. Charles' direction can function to socialize the values and norms of the group—indeed, that is often an objective.

Beyond this group-level socialization, staff are known to intervene directly in peer groups to resolve peer conflicts. The previous chapter discussed how Cheryl helped Tiffany develop social skills. As part of this effort, Cheryl on occasion talked with Tiffany's peer group to help them respond more positively to some of Tiffany's mannerisms that were off-putting. In a similar manner, because Cheryl knew these other girls well, she was able to guide Tiffany in ways to best present herself to the girls. Cheryl also engaged in this type of network consultation in support of girls who had part-time jobs or extra homework. These girls had less time available for team practices, but Cheryl persuaded the other team members to allow these girls extra flexibility so that they could manage both their club and nonclub activities.

Accordingly, adult staff can increase the potential effectiveness of their mentoring by consulting with and socializing peer friendship networks. Doing so increases the comprehensiveness, and potential power, of their effort by enhancing the extent to which the youth's peer environment will support positive development across varied life domains.

Being a Mentor

As this chapter draws to a close, a warning flag should be hoisted: Merely having adult staff in an after-school program does not necessarily translate to high-quality mentoring—or, indeed, any mentoring at all. I know of some after-school programs where adults are not actively engaged with youth; at those sites, the adults are not mentors. I doubt that many strong mentoring relationships were formed at the 21st Century Community Learning Centers, given the limited enthusiasm of teachers (the primary after-school staff) to join the program and the modest amount of time that students and staff spent at the site.[73] In each of the six clubs we studied in our research, staff functioned as mentors. However, some staff were more active in this domain than were others.

It is not always easy to determine the extent to which staff are being mentors. Much mentoring occurs one-on-one, in private. However, when we join our observations of publicly displayed mentoring with findings from interviews with youth and staff that include reports of private exchanges, it is clear that staff differ in the extent to which they affirm the identity and role of mentor. There are staff at several of these clubs who are not entirely sure of their role. We heard a number of them exclaim that they are not "counselors." These individuals tend not to be very clear about what their role should be. Although they function as mentors on occasion, they likely would be much more actively engaged and effective if they identified with that role.

For adult staff such as Charles and Cheryl, being mentors was one of the best parts of working with youth. They saw themselves as being able to pass on knowledge and wisdom. They created new vehicles (programs and activities) that enabled them to increase the time in which they could mentor and broaden the range of topics they could address. They were strongly supported in these efforts by the club director.

If after-school programs are to realize their considerable potential in mentoring, they need to be much more self-conscious about staff development in this area. This should involve explicit and repeated discussions about the importance of the role, the kinds of issues to address, and strategies that have been found to be effective with the youth that they serve. Thus, there is a parallel process that needs to work. To best foster identity development in youth, staff must maximally develop their own identity as mentors. After-school organizations need to provide supports for both processes.

CONCLUSIONS

The four sections of this chapter examined staff in their role as mentors to youth. The first section began by looking at Charles, the issues he addressed, and the methods that he used with his adolescent boys. The findings from this research were then considered with respect to consensus results reported in the literature on youth mentoring programs. The next section compared youth's relationships with club staff with youth's relationships with their most important adult kin and school adult. Finally, the chapter provided a theoretical, action-oriented framework for considering how after-school staff can mentor urban youth.

The most impressive, overarching conclusion is that youth receive exceptionally wide-ranging mentoring at these types of after-school programs.

The mentoring is conveyed via diverse methods and in different settings. In addition, the breadth of issues addressed enables staff to help youth deal with critical issues in managing multiple identities. Thus, these sites provide one-stop shopping for mentoring.

In some respects, the findings point to an even more powerful role for staff mentors than we had expected. Staff–youth relationships were more strongly linked to self-esteem than were relationships with closest kin. Strong relationships were reported among boys as well as among girls, an important consideration given how hard it is for many programs to reach low-income male teens. The fact that both our qualitative and quantitative results converged in pointing to the value of these relationships provides confidence that what we found was not an anomaly.

Although not all clubs address all the issues we described or used all of the methods, what we found across sites serves as a model of what potentially could be offered at every site. The fact that such comprehensive mentoring can be provided so efficiently argues powerfully for policymakers to support these settings.

NOTES

1. Freedman (1993).
2. Rhodes (2002).
3. Anderson (1990); Collins (1991).
4. See Ferguson (1994) for related discussion, especially concerning the importance of forming mentoring relationships with early adolescent Black boys.
5. Talking trash involves boasting about one's own abilities and qualities of play, while making scornful comments about one's opponent in these areas. It is a style of communication that is aggressive in tone and content.
6. Smitherman (1977), pp. 147–148. See also Asante (1998), on indirection.
7. Smitherman (1977), p. 156.
8. Smitherman (1977), p. 148.
9. Rhodes (2002).
10. Terrenda has a relaxed style that probably facilitated Charles' level of comfort. In addition, he likely recognized that she (like Charles) is from the South. I doubt that Charles would have talked this way with a White person of such slim acquaintance. From our observations of Charles on other occasions talking with White adults in standard English, it is clear that his use of vernacular African American English represents a choice on his part.
11. Erikson (1968).
12. Markus & Narius (1986); Youniss & Yates (1997).
13. Kohut (1977).

14. Majors & Billson (1992).

15. Spencer, Cunningham, & Swanson (1995).

16. Burton et al. (1995).

17. Blumenstein (2000); Canada (1995).

18. Anderson (1999).

19. The statistical test used was analysis of variance. We also combined the items into a reliable scale, but once again there were no significant between-club differences.

20. Rhodes (2002).

21. Freedman (1993); Hamilton & Hamilton (1992); Johnson & Sullivan (1995). Few evaluations have been published and, as Rhodes (2002) noted, methodological problems (e.g., lack of comparison groups, failure to control statistically for initial differences) make interpretation problematic.

22. DuBois, Holloway, Valentine, & Cooper (2002). Their review included a re-analysis of data reported by Grossman and Tierney (1998), frequently cited as evidence of strong mentoring effects; this reanalysis suggested that the results were less powerful than had been reported.

23. Blakely, Menon, & Jones (1995); DuBois et al. (2002); DuBois & Neville (1997); Grossman & Rhodes (2002); McLearn, Colasanto, & Schoen (1998); Rhodes (2002).

24. Cotterell (1996).

25. Grossman & Johnson (1999); DuBois & Neville (1997); Morrow & Styles (1995).

26. DuBois, Neville, Parra, & Pugh-Lilly (2002); Herrera, Sipe, & McClanahan (2000); McLearn et al. (1998); Morrow & Styles (1995); Sipe (1996).

27. Freedman (1993); Rhodes (2002).

28. There were problems at some sites in the extent to which a collaborative decision-making process was successfully implemented, but these were more with club-level rather than relationship-level decisions.

29. As noted in the previous chapter, youth development organizations have traditionally emphasized relationships between youth and staff (e.g., McLaughlin et al., 1994; Roth, Brooks-Gunn, Murray, & Foster, 1998).

30. Baumrind (1991); Maccoby & Martin (1983); Mandara (in press).

31. Findings from an evaluation of the Teen Outreach Program also bear on this thesis (Allen, Kuperminc, Philliber, & Herre, 1994). This was a school-based program that involved students in community-service activities and a classroom discussion of developmental tasks. Middle school sites that provided students with high levels of both autonomy and relatedness were significantly more successful in reducing problem behaviors. The autonomy and relatedness measure tapped overall experiences in the classroom component, with a number of items focusing on the behavior of the adult facilitator. The results are consistent with our findings, though their assessment does not permit an unambiguous comparison.

32. Roffman (2000).

33. The subcategories differ somewhat from those used by Roffman (2000).

34. Roth et al. (1998).

35. We also asked youth if there were significant nonparental adults in other spheres of their life, such as church or neighborhood, but few youth named such adults.

36. Cole (1999). The increase in violence prior to 1993 seems—in no small part—because of easy access to guns that occurred during the advent of crack cocaine and growth of inner-city drug markets (Blumenstein, 2000).

37. Buka, Stichick, Birdthistle, & Earls (2000).

38. Buka et al. (2000); Overstreet, Dempsey, Graham, & Moely (1999); Schubiner, Scott, & Tzelepis (1993).

39. Garbarino, Kostelny, & Dubrow (1991).

40. This is true even when youth–staff relationships are at the core of the research (e.g., Baker, Pollack, & Kohn, 1995).

41. We statistically controlled for a number of variables that might affect youth well-being. Some of these are fairly standard and tap potentially salient familial and neighborhood variables (i.e., parental education, parental marital status, whether the youth received free or reduced-price lunch at school, and neighborhood poverty rate). Others assess the extent of extracurricular activity, including the number of days that youth typically attended the club per week, so we know that any subsequent findings would reflect the influence of the youth-staff relationship over and above the mere rate of participation at the site.

    The final background or control variable—youth's rating of the closeness of his or her relationship with their parent (typically, their mother)—deserves special mention. Our overarching concern is with the specific impact of the youth–staff relationship, but the nature of the youth–staff relationship may reflect the effects of other youth relationships, or the youth's general relationship style. We address this concern in part by comparing youth's relationship to staff with his or her relationship with two other significant adults. By controlling for youth's closeness to his or her parent (mother), which could influence the youth's relationship with all three adults as well as youth well-being, we further strengthen our ability to tease apart the specific role of youth's relationship with club staff.

    There were a large number of control variables relative to our sample size. Accordingly, a composite variable—the unweighted sum of the background variables (all of which were coded as binary variables)—was created. Further details are provided in Pagano (2000).

42. Separate scales (with otherwise identical items) were developed for each relationship. The 11-item positive interaction (support) and 7-item negative interaction scales (rejection) were internally reliable (alphas ranged from .74 to .78 for the support measure and from .66 to .75 for the rejection measure). See Pagano (2000) for additional methodological details. The interpretation provided here differs somewhat from that provided by Pagano, given the additional qualitative data that were obtained subsequent to her report.

The self-esteem measure was taken from Owens (1994), who referred to it as positive self-worth. It consists of four items and had satisfactory internal reliability.

43. For the club adult (R^2 = .23), for closest kin (= .10), for closest tie to school adult (= .05). All R^2 figures are adjusted for sample size. Differences in R^2 at the main effect level were trivial (.10 vs .08 vs .04).

44. See Fagan and Wilkinson (1998) for an excellent analysis of the contexts and functions of adolescent violence.

45. In the evaluation of the NYC Beacons, youth frequently referred to the presence of on-site security guards (Warren et al., 2002). There were no guards at any of the clubs we studied.

46. Chaiken (1998), p. 356.

47. Maslow (1968), especially chapter 4.

48. This discussion draws heavily on Hegel's (1807/1977) analysis of the confrontation between two masters in the *Phenomenology of Spirit*.

49. See Cicchetti and Lynch (1993), and Richters and Martinez (1993) for related work on the home. Also Simmons and Blyth (1987) and Call and Mortimer (2001) on arenas of comfort.

50. See Hirsch and DuBois (1992) for discussion of relevant methodological issues in a prospective, longitudinal analyses of peer social support during the transition to junior high school.

51. For an excellent review of how poverty impacts development, see McLoyd (1998).

52. Hirsch (1981).

53. Harter (1999) would say that the identity should not be part of a "false self"; psychodynamic theorists would say that the identity should be ego syntonic.

54. Kohut (1977, 1984).

55. Strozier (2001).

56. See Larson (2000) for an extended discussion of how after-school programs, and youth development organizations more generally, can foster initiative.

57. Bandura (1986).

58. Halpern et al. (2000).

59. Rogoff (1990).

60. The classic works are by Baldwin (1895), Cooley (1902), James (1890), and Mead (1934). The basic tenet of the symbolic interactionists regarding self or identity development is that a person's self-concept reflects his or her view of how others see him or her (the "looking glass"). More recent work drawing on this tradition has been done by a number of others, including Stryker (1980; Ervin & Stryker, 2001) and, especially for our purposes, Susan Harter (1999), who extends these ideas to children and youth both theoretically and empirically.

61. See, for example, Thoits (1990) on the importance of emotional support.

62. Anderson (1999); Cross & Strauss (1998).

63. Gee (1996), p. 127.

64. Gee (1996), p. 135. Italics are in the original text.

65. Youth occasionally cursed in front of our adult research staff. In most instances, either they themselves realized that they had done something unacceptable in the club or they were reminded of that transgression by other youth nearby. An apology was typically then offered.

66. Harter (1999).

67. Bandura (1986) emphasized that observation is a fundamental mechanism of learning.

68. Harter (1999).

69. Musick (1993).

70. Stack (1974).

71. Phelan, Davidson, & Cao (1991); Phelan, Davidson, & Yu (1997).

72. Newman (1996), p. 333.

73. Dynarski et al. (2003).

II

PROGRAMS, ACTIVITIES, AND GENDER

5

STRUCTURED PROGRAMS: THE IMPLEMENTATION OF SMART GIRLS

Recreation and relationships have turned out to be core ingredients in comprehensive urban after-school organizations. What about more structured programs and activities? Should they be considered part of the core, too? Do they provide a strong enough foundation around which other activities should be designed? And how do such programs impact relationships between youth and staff—are they helpful or are they a hindrance to relationship development?

Almost by definition, comprehensive after-school centers offer a wide variety of activities that go beyond the recreational. All of these clubs offer academic assistance, computer access, leadership development activities, community service, entrepreneurial opportunities (typically food sales), field trips to museums, and so on. However, what has captured the interest of many policymakers has been structured preventive interventions. Often developed by academics, a number of these interventions have been shown to prevent problem behaviors, including poor school performance, delinquency, and psychological symptomatology, often by teaching a variety of problem-solving and socioemotional skills.[1] The overwhelming majority of these prevention programs have been school based. A much smaller number have been community based.[2]

The 2002 report by the National Research Council and Institute of Medicine (USA) (NRC/IOM) advocates increased utilization of structured, psychoeducational programs in community settings.[3] In so doing, the NRC/IOM panel does not seem to be anticipating major problems in implementation. They are attentive to the lack of implementation evaluation in prior work in this area—they repeatedly describe the extent of such research as ranging from none to very little—but this does not seem to concern them much.[4] The implicit conclusion is that implementation will not be a serious enough problem to warrant tempering their push for the development of structured programs.

If one reads the broader program implementation literature, however, a number of red flags go up immediately. Several decades of research suggest that implementation in fact will be a major problem. It is worth examining this literature to place in context our research on the clubs' implementation of a structured psychoeducational program.

Much of the initial program implementation research was conducted by social scientists on the implementation of public policy initiatives.[5] This research involved an examination of the extent to which legally mandated programs were implemented as intended (referred to as program fidelity or integrity). The overarching conclusion was that implementation problems were widespread. As Richard Elmore concluded,

> A large collection of carefully documented case studies—in education, manpower, housing, and economic development—points consistently to the same basic pattern: grand pretensions, faulty execution, puny results.[6]

A major analytic focus in these arenas has been on problems encountered in top-down approaches to policy development. In a top-down approach, executives decide on the policy to be adopted, with detailed guidelines and operating procedures formulated for field implementation. However, those working on the front lines, referred to frequently as street-level bureaucrats, often do not follow these directions or do so only in a pro forma manner. In some instances they ignore directives or try to sabotage the program. In other instances, they substantially modify the program to meet local conditions in ways that they believe will make their responsibilities manageable or enhance the program's effectiveness. Their supervisors frequently do not correct these deviations from plan, as the supervisors, too, can have conflicting reactions to the directive, too many other responsibilities, lack of sufficient expertise, and so on.

The implementation picture is not so different in respect to preventive, psychoeducational interventions. These interventions are often similar in content, and sometimes goals, to youth development programs. It is well worth examining this literature for lessons applicable to after-school centers.

Prevention programs are rarely legally mandated. Instead, they are often developed by university researchers under highly supportive conditions, conditions that typically do not obtain in most real-life settings. If outcome studies indicate that the intervention is efficacious, efforts are then made to disseminate the program as designed. This kind of strategy often does not work. As Maurice Elias, who has been at the forefront in developing preventive interventions that teach socioemotional skills, notes:

> [I]t is typically the case that innovations are established under demonstration project conditions. This implies that there are special funds, readily available materials, careful training and follow-up consultation, and the presence of evaluators on the scene to observe the work, take measures and give feedback, and involve the host site in modifying the intervention in light of the data. These special conditions create an implementation context that subsequent sites often are hard-pressed to match. The literature is replete with examples of how changes in programs during the dissemination stage led to their demise or to disappointing effectiveness. . . .[7]

Denise Gottfredson and colleagues reviewed a variety of studies that suggest that there is substantial variation in the quality of prevention implementation.[8] They conclude that only well-implemented prevention programs find positive effects, though other reviewers find the evidence less conclusive.[9] The Gottfredson group describes in detail implementation problems they themselves encountered over a 4-year period at a school that had previously hosted a successful preventive intervention. Their stark conclusion is that

> Prevention programs seldom work very well, primarily because they are not implemented as required by the underlying program theory. This is not a new finding.[10]

Given this prior history in both public policy and preventive intervention, we should not be surprised—indeed, we should expect—to find significant implementation problems as the clubs launched a structured, preventive program. At the same time, some positive outcomes of this program had not been anticipated by program designers. Our analysis of the clubs' implementation of the Smart Girls program will provide a basis for addressing the issues with which we began this chapter: the importance and fit of structured psychoeducational programs in this type of after-school setting. Accordingly, for the broader audience of readers, the importance of the extensive discussion of this one program is in examining the potential of a *type* of structured programming that currently enjoys substantial support. I think the problems encountered in implementing Smart Girls are likely to arise in implementing all kinds of structured programs in garden-variety settings for early adolescents. At the same time, some readers will be more interested in our account of the experiences of early adolescent girls in a targeted program than in generic issues in implementation. This chapter is for both groups.

SMART GIRLS

One of the core goals of the gender equity initiative was to launch new programs for girls at all of the clubs. As part of this strategy, at the beginning of the second year of the initiative the clubs were mandated by regional headquarters to implement Smart Girls. The Smart Girls program had been developed at the Boys and Girls Clubs of America national headquarters and had a 110-page manual. Thus, in both its original formulation and its specific implementation in these sites, a top-down approach was used. The ultimate goal, as stated in the program manual, was

> for girls to develop healthy attitudes and lifestyles. To accomplish this, the program addresses health and social issues that are specific to young women. **SMART Girls** is designed to prepare girls, ages 10–15, to make positive decisions at this critical stage in their physical, cognitive, emotional and social development.[11]

A total of 32 sessions were specified across five domains.[12] Lifeskills, the largest component, was similar to many existing preventive interventions in addressing a variety of problem-solving, communication, and coping skills. Know Your Body concerned physical and emotional development, examining facts and myths concerning sexuality, and addressed issues in pregnancy prevention and media influences on young females. Eating Healthy and Fitness focused on nutritional needs, exercise, and sports. Accessing the Health Care System involved guest speakers and field trips to health care settings. Role Models and Other Mentors involved developing positive attitudes toward possible adult mentors, communication skills with adults, leadership, and community service.

Each club designated a female staff person to run the program. Training consisted of a 1-day workshop; the morning session involved going over the manual and doing some role-playing, and in the afternoon session a film on teen sexuality and pregnancy was shown. Each person had a copy of the manual.

We used a variety of strategies to assess the implementation of this program. In four of the five clubs that actually implemented the program, we observed Smart Girls sessions (in one club, we observed sessions over a 2-year period). In each club, we conducted interviews with staff and youth. We also attended a staff training session and I discussed implementation issues with the director of the gender equity initiative, who conducted her own observations.

I first summarize positive features of the program and then implementation problems. I then take a much closer look at how Smart Girls functioned at one particular club.

Positive Features

Prior to the gender equity initiative, there were few girls-only programs and one of the goals of the initiative was to launch programs that would attract the interest of girls. In this respect, Smart Girls was generally a success. Girls attended regularly and participated with some enthusiasm. In a few clubs it took a number of months for this to occur, but once a reasonably committed staff member was put in place who convened the group on a reasonably regular basis, girls participated. Thus, the group was able to generate sufficient motivation for girls to become actively engaged in the program activities.

Many of the sessions we observed were from the Lifeskills component. The girls seemed to learn one of the main lessons of that section, the importance of talking with concerned adults when serious problems arose. At the West River Club, for instance, an early adolescent girl found herself in a potentially threatening sexual situation outside of the club. After she told some of her friends, the girls insisted she talk about this to club staff, and the language they used in advising her sounded as though it came straight out of Smart Girls sessions.

At two of the clubs, the women who ran Smart Girls had especially good mentoring relationships with the girls in the group. The curricula appeared to provide a context that promoted the development of these relationships. Such a relationship is an important potential benefit and we shall consider this in some depth later in the chapter.

Thus, although we did not formally evaluate program outcomes, some positive potential was evident at most of the sites. At the same time, there were many problems in implementation, some of them serious.[13]

Implementation Problems Across the Clubs

Basic Treatment Integrity

Sabotage is something that needs to be considered in any study of implementation, especially when a top-down strategy is adopted.[14] We found a clear instance of sabotage at the New City Club. Linda had started a Girls Council at the club, which involved girls in planning activities. When she received the order to begin a Smart Girls group, she changed the name of the group: "I renamed the group Smart Girls to satisfy paperwork requirements. . . ." She did modify the focus of the group to incorporate some Smart Girls activities: "[W]e would do both sex ed and things like an end-of-year trip." However, by no stretch of the imagination could this be considered an implementation of the full Smart Girls program. The gap between the program as designed and what was implemented was so profound that it amounted to a breach of the basic integrity of the program.

Dosage

Dosage refers to how much of the specified activities were actually provided. Dosage was a major problem at all of the clubs. At every club, meetings were frequently postponed or cancelled, often with little warning. This was not something specific to Smart Girls, but rather was how most club programs operated. Sometimes a staff member had to be reassigned because another staff member had called in sick; however, it was not always possible to determine the reason for cancellations. The meetings sometimes did take place later in the week; the fact that most children were there almost every day made this kind of flexibility possible. Nevertheless, some youth perceived failures to meet as reflecting a lack of commitment or seriousness on the part of staff, which decreased their own motivation for the program.[15]

There were several additional dosage-type problems. Several of the Lifeskills sessions were designed to be conducted sequentially, but this did not always occur. Regardless of the focus area, all sessions were supposed to end with youth either making a journal entry or discussing the point they had learned in the session. Presumably this would help highlight and integrate the salient lessons. Yet this was done at one site only.

Staff Skillfulness

The Lifeskills sessions were generally designed to start with a dramatic reading of an ongoing story and some sessions involved role-playing. These more challenging type of activities were rarely done well. The readings were often perfunctory and the role-plays never appeared to simulate real-life circumstances.

Some staff began the session by thumbing through the manual and picking out which session appealed to them at the moment. They would thus run the session without any prior preparation.

A few staff encountered difficulties in managing group dynamics. At times, this caused the session to degenerate into conflict.

I should note that these kind of quality control problems would not necessarily be identified in the kind of quantitative, questionnaire assessment that is often conducted in implementation research (when implementation is examined at all). In all of these instances, the group leader could legitimately check off an activity as having been conducted (dosage), without any clear way for the evaluator to realize the lack of skillfulness that had been displayed. Indeed, a comprehensive review of prevention evaluation studies published between 1980 and 1994 found that only 7% measured quality of delivery at all.[16]

Training and Supervision

Prior studies have documented that one of the major difficulties in program implementation is the inadequate time devoted to training and supervision. The literature makes it clear not only that substantial amounts of time need to be allocated to training staff prior to delivering the intervention, but that additional training and supervision needs to be provided over the course of the intervention.[17]

Smart Girls training consisted entirely of a 1-day workshop. As noted, only half of that workshop dealt with program sessions. The workshop leaders, moreover, although highly skilled in working with youth, had themselves never conducted any Smart Girls sessions. There was thus a clear limit to what they could teach, even if they had the time. There were no follow-up workshops. There was no supervision. Nor did program staff or potential supervisors have a reservoir of relevant knowledge that they could draw on.[18] Yes, all of them had experience in working with youth, but this was the first structured psychoeducational program these particular staff had ever run at the clubs. Indeed, in the several years prior to the gender equity initiative, little staff training of any sort had been provided.

Although the amount of training for Smart Girls was minimal, it is not entirely out of line with what has been reported even for well-funded federal programs.[19] The lack of supervision is also far from unprecedented: Only 40% of published prevention evaluation studies reported that supervision was provided by personnel who had experience in implementing the program.[20] Given that published evaluation studies probably focus more rigorously on quality of implementation, I would imagine that the extent of supervision is even less in run-of-the-mill prevention programs. Thus, training and supervisory limitations are real and need to be factored into strategic thinking about how best to strengthen programs, but these problems are far from specific to these Boys & Girls clubs or to after-school centers more generally.

I now turn to examine in detail the implementation of Smart Girls at one site. Such case material is essential to develop a deep understanding of the strengths and limitations of these programs. A shared, concrete basis is needed for discussing the seriousness of those limitations, for drawing realistic conclusions about what programs can accomplish, and for aiding designers in considering how best to realize the potential of programs in actual field sites.

SMART GIRLS AT THE CLEMENTE CLUB

For several years, the Clemente club had sought without success to recruit adolescent girls to a variety of different programs. Toward the beginning of the third year of the gender equity initiative, Aurelia, a popular twentysomething front-desk clerk, was promoted and directed to begin offering Smart Girls as well as develop a Girls Council. She gathered around her a group of eight Latina girls, ages 11 and 12, who spoke to us with pride and enthusiasm of their participation in Smart Girls. I have chosen to focus on this particular group because among the group leaders at the different clubs, Aurelia ranked the highest on treatment integrity and her group illustrates well both the problems and the potential of structured psychoeducational programs in these types of after-school settings. Field notes from two sessions in consecutive weeks are presented. At each session, two research assistants were in attendance; both had a good working knowledge of Spanish, although that was rarely needed during these sessions.

Session 1: Truth or Myth

The notes on this session are presented verbatim, then discussed. The Truth or Myth session comes from the Know Your Body section of Smart Girls.

> Aurelia sat behind the desk and all the girls pulled up chairs around it, only using up about one third of the space. They start off by role call, in which everyone signed in on the sheet. . . . Aurelia flipped through her book [the manual] and asked if the girls wanted to play a game. At once everyone said yes. Then Aurelia explained that some of the girls had already played this game and that it was called Truth or Myth. A few of the girls recognized it and Estephanie said, "Oh, I got first place in the game," followed by Rosa who said, "I got second." . . . The only one who wasn't jumping out of her seat and ready to go was Maria, who never played the game and didn't know what was going on.
>
> Aurelia gave each girl a sheet of paper with an M on one side and a T on the other side [myth or truth]. Then we all went into the auditorium where there was more room to play. The object of the game was to correctly state if the statements that Aurelia presented were true or if they were a myth. If you answered correctly, you moved forward. The first one to reach the stage was the winner. It took Aurelia about 5 minutes to get everyone to stand against the far wall and then she began. Aurelia would read the statement, which all had to do with sex or the female reproductive system, and then the girls would show their answers. Those who got it correct would move forward. At times it would take someone some time to answer the question, usually because they were confused about the statement. Three or four times Angelica just stared at Aurelia, with her hands on her hips and an expression saying "I don't know and I don't care." Aurelia would then try to explain,

but the girls would all get upset and bored. "Come on, Aurelia, just read the question." Maribel, one of the girls who came later, had pulled up a chair and was spinning around. Estephanie and Rosa were screaming at anyone who they thought moved forward when they weren't supposed to and calling them a cheater. Towards the end of the game no one was listening and they would randomly put their sign up. When 5 o'clock came around, they all ran out of the auditorium and back downstairs to the table with food. Aurelia just looked at us and smiled.

Despite generally following the curricular guide and having had prior experience with this particular session, Aurelia was unable to manage the group dynamics and the session deteriorated profoundly. At the beginning, she never clearly defined the objective. Yes, she correctly pointed out that they would be doing a race, but she did not inform them that the "focus will be on finding out some true facts about sex." They did not "as a group, determine if there is any truth to the statement," nor did she "ask the girls to share some of the sexual myths they have heard" or "reinforce the idea that there are a lot of rumors and statements made about sex and sexual behavior that are not true."[21] The focus on the race per se proved disastrous as some girls never quite understood what was going on, others became bored, and competitiveness began to rule. It is doubtful that any learning took place.

Session 2: Lifeskills

This next session proved more successful, though there were still problems. The curriculum guide was followed, but important elements were omitted. An unanticipated disclosure by one of the girls highlights potential benefits of the program beyond those suggested by the program manual.

These field notes are more extensive and, to best detail what occurred, I have mixed together notes from the two researchers (Didi and Nadia) who participated in the group.

The topic of today's Smart Girls was decision making, what it means and how to do it. As part of the activity, the girls read a little story and then answered some questions about the situation that was described. Aurelia said that there were three parts to the exercise which would take about an hour each, but she would try to do most of it today.

Karina read the narrative, which was a quote from a fictional figure, Tanya, a 15-year-old girl who was talking about family problems. She had two older sisters who left home when they turned 17; one of them was pregnant. She said that she didn't want to end up like that but maybe she would. Her father was always drinking at bars and had a bad temper, and her mother, Jill, had been going out a lot and hanging out with a new "friend," Jack. She had two younger siblings whom she had to take care of all the time, so she never got to go out. She had made a new friend at school, Sara, who had a nice house and lots of nice clothes and hung out at the mall. She had asked her to go to the mall, but Tanya couldn't go because she had to stay with her siblings. Her friend has asked her to go to a wild party soon, and Tanya said she was going no matter what, and her mom had said that she could.

Aurelia asked Karina to read it, or act it out, since she was the oldest; however, she was very reluctant to do so. First, Karina went down to make copies so that everyone could follow along while she read. Then she went down to get Nadia and me [Didi] some water. Then Alejandra went down to get some pop for herself and Maribel. After everyone was back in the room and waiting for Karina to start, her chair slipped into a small hole in the floor and she fell. She got up and then put her head on the table, trying to procrastinate as much as possible. Someone else offered to read and, when she heard that, Karina popped her head up and began reading. She started reading the first paragraph. Someone else asked to read the next paragraph . . . Karina said sure but simply continued to read without stopping to give someone else a chance.

Everyone participated and tried to share their answers [to questions posed by Aurelia from the manual]. Some questions were simply taken out of the story, such as the first question. The answer to this question ["Do you really think no one cares about Tanya?"] was taken straight from the third paragraph of the anecdote. At one point Maribel was trying to answer the questions or give her opinion, but no one would let her as they continued to speak over her. Angelica noticed and told everyone to be quiet so that Maribel could talk. Everyone immediately went quiet and waited for Maribel to finish what she had to say. . . .

When the group came to the second question on the sheet ["What do you think Tanya should or could do about her father who drinks too much?"], one of the girls suggested that Tanya should go and talk to someone, such as a school counselor, about what is going on in her house. Maria immediately started shaking her head no. "The counselors tell the principal everything. I would rather talk with Aurelia than with a counselor," she said. She followed this with a short example of a friend of hers who had problems at home and went to talk to the school counselor. Later, somehow the principal knew about what was going on and talked to her. Maria then got really quiet and looked down at the table. Aurelia sat back in her chair and said, "Well," and looked toward the other girls. They said that their counselor didn't do that, and Maria said, "Mine does." Then Aurelia said something about that's what counselors are there for. [She seemed not to know what to say. . . .] Aurelia then asked whom the girls go to if they have a problem. Maria mentioned her grandmother, while Karina mentioned her aunt. The other girls agreed that if they couldn't go to their parents then they went to some other family member.

To the next question ["Do you think having a nice house and nice clothes are everything?"], all the girls chimed in, "Nooo." Aurelia asked why, and one of the girls said, "Because the mom might be drinking all the time, and the dad might be gone all the time." Aurelia said, "Yeah, they might still have the same problems." They all chimed in, "Yeah."

As the group was talking and going over the questions, someone knocked on the door. Alejandra answered it and everyone became silent as they saw who was there. It was the girl who had just turned 13 and so was now a part of another group. She pulled Alejandra outside to talk to her. When the door closed, they all groaned and had disappointed looks on their faces. The girls explained to us [the researchers] that ever since she turned 13, she didn't talk with them and didn't come to the groups anymore.

When Alejandra came back in after only a couple of minutes, the other girls wanted to know what was going on and what it was she wanted. Alejandra kept saying "nothing" in Spanish, and only about after the fifth time were the other girls satisfied that nothing really happened and left Alejandra alone.

[At this point, Aurelia shares with the group the fact that she will be leaving for a few weeks to help with her sister's new baby, who is ill. There is a discussion as to whether anyone else will take over the group while Aurelia is gone.]

Toward the end of the session, the girls started getting out of their seats and started wandering around the room. Maria said, "Aurelia, can I ask now?" Aurelia said, "Oh, yeah. Hold on. Maria has a question." Maria said, "It's just for pretend." We nodded. She continued, saying, "What if my mom's boyfriend came over at night and my mom didn't know we were awake . . . ." Angelica said, "Oh!" and giggled, cupping her hand over her mouth. Maria said, "It's just for pretend. [She looked at Aurelia, Didi, and I {Nadia}, and we all nodded.] She continued, "We see him in the morning. But what if my mom didn't know we were awake and we heard sex noises at night. . . . Is that natural?" There were a couple more giggles, which we [the adults] ignored. I [in the remainder of this note, Nadia is the authorial "I"] asked, "Do you mean is it natural for the mom to be having her boyfriend over, or do you mean is it natural for you to hear it?" As I finished asking about the second scenario, she started nodding and said "Yeah." Didi said, "Does it make you feel uncomfortable?" (Maria nodded quickly and grimaced.) "You should talk to her then," and Aurelia and I echoed her. Maria said, "It's just for pretend." I said, "Oh, I know." I said, "Yeah, the mom probably doesn't even know they can hear her, so she would probably be kinda embarrassed if she knew and would try not to do it. But if the kid was too embarrassed to talk to the mom about it, maybe he could say something like, 'I heard something weird last night, but I don't know what it was' and then she [the mom] know that they heard it and she might stop." Aurelia said, "Yeah, she could do that. The mom might not do it in the house then." Aurelia added that the girl should talk to someone, even if it wasn't the mom. Aurelia asked Maria if that answered her question, and Maria nodded. The girls started to get up and walk around, and a couple of them picked up stuffed animals of Tweetie Bird and Bugs Bunny that were as tall as they were.

A consideration of the different aspects of this session follows.

Early Adolescents and Structure

This group consisted of early adolescents, a fact poignantly brought to bear by the way in which they sought out their stuffed animals after discussing issues of sexuality. Between and betwixt childhood and adulthood, they bravely explore the new world while clinging to familiar comforts for sooth-ing and security. It should not be surprising if their developmental issues also influenced how effectively a structured intervention was implemented.

Developmental constraints on implementation are noticeable at the very beginning of the session. The group is designed to begin with a dramatic reading, or acting out, of the story of Tanya and Sara. Presumably, such a dramatic reading will facilitate identification and affective involvement with the characters and their issues, and help focus attention on the issues to be raised by the group leader. The manual suggests having an older girl or peer leader read the introductory material. In asking Karina (a leader among the girls, though on the quiet side) to do this, Aurelia is following the manual.[22] However, like many young people at this age, Karina is quite self-conscious about public reading and does her best to procrastinate as long as possible. This takes up a good deal of time. When she finally does read the material, she does so in a perfunctory manner with minimal affect. The other girls in the group get frustrated and annoyed. So the group begins in a manner quite opposite from what was intended.

Peer-group dynamics take the girls off-task later in the session, with the mysterious appearance of the high-status older girl. Peer-group issues are highly salient at this age (see chap. 2) and Aurelia, probably wisely, lets the girls deal with this issue for a few minutes rather than attempting to force their attention back to the assigned material. The girls deal with the incident and their hurt feelings and refocus on the session. Nevertheless, the minutes spent off-task have increased and by now are a significant portion of the designated 60 minutes. Given the amount of material that is supposed to be covered, it will be impossible to complete the material in the remainder of the session. The manual appears to be task oriented, but the girls are more oriented to interpersonal process. When something comes up, as it almost inevitably does, fewer tasks are covered and the prescribed dosage is less.

The School Counselor Discussion

One of the objectives of the session is to have the girls apply what hap-pens to Tanya and Sara to their own lives, "to consider what participants might do if they were in this situation."[23] The manual does not provide any guidance as to how the group leader should accomplish this; it does specify that girls should discuss the advantages and disadvantages of Tanya talking to her parents about how she feels, for example, but says nothing about how to transition into a discussion of how this applies to their own real-life issues. Thus, even if the group leader wanted to maximize treatment fidelity, it is not at all clear how to do so in this (and many similar) instances.

Fortunately, Maria brings the fictional material into the girls' personal space by discussing how a school counselor breached confidentiality with one of her friends. A lively give-and-take ensues. Other adults, especially female kin, are identified as resources and support figures. This discussion enabled one of the objectives of the session to be fulfilled, but the manner in which it was accomplished was fortuitous.

Mom's Sex Life

One of the more memorable moments from this session came when Maria brought up, "for pretend," the episode in which her mom made sex noises at night with the mom's boyfriend. This is a highly personal, intimate topic and it says a lot about the trust in the group that Maria was able to raise this issue. Maria had indicated beforehand to Aurelia that she had something she wanted to talk about. As Maria told our researchers after this meeting, she considered Smart Girls to be "when we could talk about things with Aurelia that we don't want to talk about with others. It's about puberty and stuff," so it made sense that she would raise this kind of topic during a Smart Girls meeting. This provides another opportunity to discuss decision making in these girls' lives, a central feature of the Lifeskills unit, though again nothing in the manual suggests how this might be done; indeed, Aurelia was about to end the meeting when Maria reminded her that she had something she wanted to bring up.

In responding to Maria's "pretend" inquiry about the mother's sex noises, the two researchers in the group functioned too much as participants and not enough as observers (which we discussed during our supervisory session). Aurelia did make a number of comments to Maria, but she might have made more, and of a different sort, had not the two researchers jumped in first. Without seeking to justify the researchers' behavior, I will use it as an opportunity to reflect on Aurelia's skillfulness in the group. There was reason to wonder whether Aurelia would make much of a response to Maria's self-disclosure. Aurelia had responded minimally and with confusion to Maria's earlier remarks about counselor violation of confidentiality. In the prior week's session on truth and myth, Aurelia had consistently demonstrated difficulty in managing group process and in responding with any elaboration to issues of sexual behavior. Given the sensitive nature of Maria's remarks, an intensive reply was needed, and there was good reason to doubt that Aurelia would provide this. What Aurelia did say gave guidance and reassurance. There is little question that Aurelia provides a very warm and supportive presence in the lives of these girls (more on this shortly). However, the depth of her guidance is open to question.

Curricular Coverage

In terms of covering the designated material for this session, Aurelia would receive a mixed mark. On the positive side, she presented the initial portions of Tanya's and Sara's adventures verbatim and explicitly raised a number of questions posed in the manual. The importance of talking to adults about problems was emphasized and there was some application to the girls' own social network.

There also were a number of weaknesses in Aurelia's coverage of the material. Aurelia asked fewer than half the questions for this session. Many of the unaddressed questions were designed to foster discussions of the advantages and disadvantages of different choices, which might promote a deeper understanding of the issues and of the decision-making process. She also did not summarize and integrate the material at the end of the session as instructed. Given that Aurelia did not cover much of the material for the session, her statement at the beginning of the meeting that she would in fact finish this and two subsequent sessions in 1 hour suggests that her understanding of the program is severely limited. It should be recalled that one of the reasons I selected Aurelia for an in-depth analysis was that among Smart Girls leaders, she was the one most concerned with treatment fidelity; other leaders tended to cover even less of the material.

Overall, the weaknesses of this session centered on the extent of curricular coverage, the skillfulness with which some elements were implemented (e.g., the initial reading of the story), and the depth of coverage of topics. The strength of the session had to do with interpersonal process. Maria felt comfortable raising a highly personal issue with Aurelia and with her peers. Group cohesion was probably increased both by dealing with this issue and by the solidarity with which they confronted the intrusion of the older girl. The girls also considered other adults (especially kin) whom they could talk to and discussed the variability among school counselors in responding to confidential material. The ease with which Aurelia dealt with these various matters probably strengthened her bond with the girls. She did not cover some issues to as great an extent as might be desirable from a didactic perspective, but the girls may well have processed and integrated as much material as they could for a 60-minute meeting. Given the importance of these process dimensions to evaluating this session, and Smart Girls more generally, it is worth considering these variables in more detail.

Nonspecific Treatment Effects

In the psychotherapy literature, there is considerable debate over whether treatment effects are specific or nonspecific. Specific effects refer to those that can be attributed to a procedure that is distinctive to a particular treatment approach—for example, transference interpretations in psychodynamic therapy, and repeated rehearsal in cognitive behavioral approaches. By contrast, nonspecific effects refer to those that are due to procedures that are common across approaches. Among the more important nonspecific effects are those that involve positive features of the therapeutic relationship (e.g., therapist warmth and empathy), and the fact that therapy enables clients to devote focused attention to their problems and their amelioration.[24] Some of the points raised by the nonspecific argument appear to apply to our consideration of Smart Girls.

The Smart Girls curriculum was implemented very imperfectly at Clemente (and the other clubs), but girls seemed to benefit from the focused attention devoted to important issues and from the deeper relationship they developed with Aurelia. We talked to each of the Clemente Smart Girls after Aurelia left to take care of her sister's baby and it is clear that the girls appreciated the opportunity to talk about puberty, sexuality, and other personal topics that they were unlikely to discuss with other adults. The sessions enabled them to talk about highly personal things that concerned them. They could express confusions and doubts (as Maria did about the "pretend" mother) and receive feedback on values and preferred behavior. Although Aurelia had a very incomplete understanding of the curricula and did not implement many of the procedures skillfully, the girls had developed a very positive relationship with her.

> *We used to talk to her all about what happened in school and about problems.*
> —Karina

> *We trusted her and she was a great friend. She was really fun . . . We had a lot of parties, especially birthday parties.*
> —Samantha

> *We could talk to her if we had problems or something. She would always understand our problems.*
> —Angelica

> *[W]e learned about sex and periods. And don't let a boy touch you or let anyone do anything to you . . . I feel better when I tell her how I feel.*
> —Maria

> *She taught us stuff we didn't know. They let us keep the stuffed animals because she asked.*
> —Maribel

> *She was like our mom. She tried to help us.*
> —Estephanie

> *[S]he taught us to be careful, if we didn't want to have a baby, and about HIV. She would be like a mom because whenever it was our birthday, she gave us a surprise party.*
> —Rosa

> *We got to talk. She was like somebody special to us.*
> —Alejandra

In thinking back about their time with Aurelia, the girls do not refer to the curricular elements of Smart Girls—to the story of Tanya and Sara, the Truth or Myth game, and so on. Instead, they recall with affection Aurelia's personal qualities and how she acted toward them. Her openness and responsiveness to their problems. The guidance she provided. Her caring and appreciation. Her advocacy. How she celebrated their birthdays. These are relationships characterized by sharing, enjoyment, and tenderness. Aurelia, like Charles, was a true mentor, helping the girls navigate through early adolescence. The time they spent together in Smart Girls enhanced nonspecifics—their relationship and attention to developmental issues—more so than accomplishing the specific procedures of the program manual.[25]

The importance of the relationship that program participants form with adult leaders has been noted in other evaluations of youth development programs. Findings from the Quantum Opportunities Program are of special interest, as this program was identified as one of three especially promising initiatives by the 2002 NRC/IOM report. Quantum Opportunities provided an array of services for high school students from families receiving public assistance in several cities. The program design included educational activities (e.g., tutoring, computer-based instruction), service activities (e.g., community service), developmental activities (e.g., curricula focused on life/family skills), and financial stipends (totaling several thousand dollars). Clear differences emerged among the sites in their ability to implement these services. Although the initial design emphasized formal programs, the evaluators focused on the role of youth–staff ties in contributing to positive outcomes:

> The most optimistic finding of this study is that teenagers are able to benefit significantly even when formal group services provided to them are modest. If young people are connected with caring adults for sustained periods of time, year-round, positive results do emerge (Hahn, Leavitt, & Aaron, 1994, p. 16).

Thus, as in our analysis of Smart Girls, the evaluation of Quantum Opportunities documented not only substantial problems in program implementation, but also the importance of nonspecific factors, particularly the youth–staff relationship. These similarities emerged even though Smart Girls and Quantum Opportunities differed substantially in program design, host organization, age and gender of participants, length (Quantum lasted for 4 years), and so on. Given the scarcity of research on after-school programs, the consistency of these findings despite numerous program differences is noteworthy.

CONCLUSION

There were significant problems in implementing Smart Girls, but this should not come as much of a surprise, given extensive documentation of problems in implementing a wide range of social programs, including structured psychoeducational programs with preventive goals. The NRC/IOM report, by its failure to adequately consider the likelihood of such problems, opens the door to "blaming" sites that encounter difficulties. It would be most unfortunate if research studies such as this are used to play the blame game. Implementation problems are universal, and not just in youth programs or schools, but almost in every place society works with complex social issues. We do need to acknowledge limitations, but we are more likely to move forward if we can do so in a problem-solving mode that is both sympathetic and tough-minded.

We began this chapter by posing the question whether structured psychoeducational programs should be a foundational element of comprehensive urban after-school programs. Our analysis of Smart Girls, at both Clemente and the other clubs, argues against viewing such programs as a foundation or core strength on which other activities can be constructed. Structured programs, when run by engaging and committed staff, did attract youth interest and participation. Yet several of the staff who were assigned to the program had little commitment to it. Even among committed staff, there were serious problems in implementation, resulting in part from inadequate training and in part from the culture of the clubs. Weak training and nonexistent supervision resulted in insufficient understanding of the program, haphazard preparation, modest coverage of session material, and poor execution of many procedures. The culture of the club led to many sessions that were postponed or cancelled, weakening commitment and decreasing treatment dosage. Given these factors, as well as significant staff turnover, it is difficult to see how Smart Girls or other structured programs would improve dramatically over time, if at all. It does not seem wise to build a foundation around something that is not done particularly well.

Advocates of structured programs might make two counterarguments to this position. Both arguments raise serious issues that merit attention.

The first counterargument is that after-school programs ought to devote considerably more resources to training and supervision so that structured programs such as Smart Girls will be implemented much more successfully. I certainly agree that increased training and supervision would improve implementation. The question is, How realistic is it to expect this to happen? The amount of training needed would be substantial and ongoing, 2 to 3 dozen hours at a minimum. Additional training would need to be provided to supervisors so that they could do an effective job. On the basis of their work with school-based programs, Gottfredson and colleagues make a similar argument about the extensiveness of needed training, which is much more than would typically be devoted to any other school program.[26] Given extensive turnover among staff and supervisors, the costs would be recurring rather than one-time-only. It is extremely difficult to imagine poorly funded after-school sites devoting such large, ongoing funds to any one such project, especially given the many competing needs that have significant constituencies.[27]

The second counterargument is that I have focused too much on whether each and every aspect of the program is implemented. What is important, it might be argued, is whether the core of the program has been successfully implemented. This view would be more influential if it were easy to determine what is core and what is not. Such a determination can be made empirically—the research designs for doing this are well known—but is rarely done.[28] Given that much of the impetus for adopting structured programs comes from empirical demonstrations of their efficacy, the absence of empirical evidence for identifying the program core substantially weakens the argument for adopting such programs. In the absence of empirical data, I am afraid that the program manual becomes another postmodern text for which any number of competing readings (interpretations) may be asserted. For example, I have repeatedly examined the manual's presentation of the second session at Clemente, presented in some detail earlier in the chapter, and am unable to clearly determine the core procedures for that session (this is far from the only session characterized by such ambiguity). This lack of clarity is not unusual; many prevention manuals are not specific enough to allow for this type of determination.[29] In the absence of convincing empirical data or theoretical analysis, I suspect that evaluating whether the core has been implemented would be operationalized in terms of a specified percentage of program content, but such a solution is unlikely to be greeted with great enthusiasm. Such modifications, moreover, are quite insufficient to justify considering such programs as foundational.

Smart Girls did have value and added to the developmental potential of these after-school sites. Yet rather than value being found in specific technical procedures, the value was in its nonspecific effects. It focused attention on important issues and provided guidance on how to deal with them. It socialized peer friendship groups to positive goals and interpersonal behavior. Most important, it provided a context in which staff could become better mentors. By focusing on a range of issues, values, and behaviors, the program enabled staff such as Aurelia to extend the range of their mentoring beyond that which they might otherwise have provided.

Charles had come to a similar conclusion. We presented his story in some detail in chapter 4. Charles had the potential to be an exceptional mentor, but dealing just with sports in the gym limited his possibilities. So he began his own program, focused on adolescent guys, though a few girls would pop in as well from time to time. The program provided a context for him to address a wider range of issues and developmental needs, in varied venues. Rather than using prepackaged material, Charles created his own, including videotapes of controversial talk shows and movies.

Prepackaged program materials, such as those in Smart Girls, can help staff operate psychoeducational programs that enable them to extend their mentoring. Charles, who was highly motivated, could have used some help in not having to develop all of his own material. Other staff, not quite so highly motivated, could probably use even more assistance. Having program material, or curricula, readily available has a number of benefits. Staff do not have to constantly create material entirely from scratch. The packaged material can provide fresh ideas for how to address issues. The variety can add freshness and help to sustain motivation among both staff and youth participants. These attractions increase the likelihood that programs will be implemented and that staff mentoring can more fully realize its potential.

Although not to be considered a foundation of urban after-school programs, packaged program material or curricula can add value. The material needs to be designed so that it can be used flexibly and be adapted to local conditions and the idiosyncrasies of diverse group leaders. The program material needs to be designed in ways that complement and blend into the culture of the site, rather than fight against it. And most important, the design should have as its overarching focus how best to enhance mentoring, rather than didactic coverage of content. A central argument of this book is that mentoring is one of the core strengths of these comprehensive after-school sites. If that argument is correct, then structured programs should build on and enhance that foundation.

Comprehensive after-school programs are well aware of the importance of the relationship between staff and youth, but this awareness was not applied to Smart Girls: Absolutely nowhere in the manual is there reference to the relationship between the group leader and the girls. Youth–staff relationships and structured programs seem to exist in separate worlds. Strategic principles for integrating these different resources and tapping the larger potential of after-school programs are discussed more fully in the concluding chapter.

NOTES

1. See reviews by Catalano et al. (1999); Durlak and Wells (1997, 1998); Greenberg, Domitrovich, and Bumbarger (1999).

2. See Roth et al. (1998) for a review of those that are community based. It should also be noted that a number of the school-based programs have a community component (see Catalano et al., 1999).

3. National Research Council and Institute of Medicine (2002).

4. A similar lack of attention to likely implementation difficulties has characterized other government reports, such as Healthy People 2000 (Elias, 1997).

5. The following discussion draws especially on Berman (1980); Brehm and Gates (1997); Elmore (1978, 1982); Fullan (1991); Lester, Bowman, Goggin, and O'Toole (1987); Linder and Peters (1987); Matland (1995); McLaughlin (1991); O'Toole (1986); Palumbo and Callista (1990); and Sabatier (1986).

6. Elmore (1978), p. 186.

7. Elias (1997), p. 262. Similarly, Lisbeth Schorr, on programs to break the cycle of disadvantage: "Agonizingly familiar is the story of a successful program which is continued or replicated in a form so diluted that the original concept is destroyed" (1989, p. 275).

8. Gottfredson (2001); Gottfredson, Fink, Skroban, & Gottfredson (1997); Gottfredson, Gottfredson, & Skroban (1998). See also Domitrovich and Greenberg (2000); Weissberg (1990).

9. Dane and Schneider (1998) comprehensively reviewed published prevention studies from 1980 to 1994; they are less persuaded that a relation between program integrity and outcome has been established. Many findings, in the few studies that examine this relation, have had nonsignificant findings. Most of the significant findings come from studies conducted by Gilbert Botvin and colleagues on their own Life Skills Training program (and these are the ones most cited by the Gottfredson group). See also Durlak (1998).

10. Gottfredson et al. (1997), p. 219.

11. Boys & Girls Clubs of America (1997), p. 6, emphasis is in the original. The manual goes on to list a variety of goals, in terms of both positive development and prevention.

12. Some sessions had two to four meetings of 1 hour each. If one counts sessions by number of meetings, then there were at least 38 sessions (a precise figure cannot be provided, as the number of sessions devoted to accessing the health care system can vary).

13. In a study of 10 urban youth agencies, Halpern et al. (2000, especially pp. 495–497) report similar implementation problems for structured programs of any type (they do not specifically examine manual-driven programs).

14. Brehm & Gates (1997).

15. See Fine and Mechling (1993) on the importance to youth that adults take the activity seriously.

16. Dane & Schneider (1998).

17. Berman & McLaughlin (1978); Fullan (1991); Halpern (1992); Robertson (1997).

18. This is a general problem in policy implementation that is not limited to psychoeducational programs, as many supervisors have only limited familiarity with the idiosyncrasies of specific tasks and procedures (e.g., Brehm & Gates, 1997).

19. Berman & McLaughlin (1978) indicate that one-session, predelivery workshops are not unusual in school reform initiatives. Even if significantly more training had been provided, it may still not have been enough. Gottfredson et al. (1998) note that although their staff received what was considered extensive training in their school district, it was still below what had been provided in the university-based demonstration project.

20. Dane & Schneider (1998). They reviewed 162 evaluations published in a limited number of journals. In a wider ranging review, Durlak (1997) found that fewer than 5% of over 1,200 published prevention studies provided

implementation data, so it is likely that the Dane and Schneider figure is an overestimation.

21. All quotes are from Boys & Girls Clubs of America (1997), p. 48.

22. The manual also suggests having a girl from the Keystone Club do the reading, specifying that all members of that group "are interested in drama or acting." I found this confusing, as none of the Keystone groups in these clubs included any work in drama or acting.

23. Boys & Girls Clubs of America (1997), p. 19.

24. Jerome Frank authored the classic works on the nonspecific argument (e.g., Frank, 1973; Frank & Frank, 1991). More recent work includes Lambert (1992), Weinberger (1995), and, especially, the edited volume by Hubble, Duncan, & Miller (1999).

25. McLaughlin et al. (1994) also emphasize the role of nonspecifics in community-based youth development organizations.

26. Gottfredson et al. (1998).

27. Kaltreider and St. Pierre (1995) discuss the extraordinary steps that Boys & Girls Clubs needed to take to implement a drug prevention program. It seems highly unlikely that staff would have continued these efforts just on behalf of this one program, given competing interests, especially as staff changed and new staff came with their own priorities and desire to make their own distinctive contributions. McLaughlin (1991) came to a similar conclusion in reviewing lessons learned from a wide variety of implementation studies: "Today's program consequences often are eroded by tomorrow's realities—staff moving on to new positions, different program clientele, changed resource availability, competing demands for time and attention." (p. 193)

28. Institute of Medicine (1994).

29. Dane & Schneider (1998).

6

GENDER WARS IN THE GYM

There is an old adage in psychology that the best way to understand a phenomenon is by trying to change it. We were fortunate to have this kind of opportunity to elaborate our understanding of after-school programs when the clubs launched a major gender equity initiative. For most of the 20th century, these were Boys Clubs, and it has been less than 2 decades since they officially became co-ed. The leadership at this Boys & Girls Clubs regional affiliate had concluded that more needed to be done for girls. So they launched a 3-year initiative, which involved, among other actions, hiring a project director, developing a series of gender sensitivity training workshops for staff, establishing liaisons with community groups interested in girls development, and encouraging the development of new programs, especially for early adolescent girls. This chapter takes a second look at recreational activities at the sites in terms of what we learned from evaluating the gender equity initiative. As documented in chapter 2, physical activity took first place when youth listed their favorite activity at the club. Moreover, as discussed, recreational activities play a critical role in recruitment, retention, and program development. Opportunities for quality recreation are therefore of fundamental importance to after-school centers.

This chapter is coauthored by Nancy Deutsch.

The gym is one of the most important places in an indoor recreational facility, but girls were frequently not made to feel at home there. If these sites were to be gender equitable, then the gym would be an important battleground. On the basis of a 3-year analysis of developments at one club, we trace the struggles, attempted solutions, and remaining tensions in transforming the gym into a girl-friendly place.[1]

EQUITY IN SPORTS

Comprehensive after-school programs are not alone in the challenges they face in creating gender-equitable sports opportunities. Although recreational activity has been part of female education since the 19th century,[2] girls' sports participation has been historically constrained by traditional gender norms, stereotypes, and discrimination. In 1972, the federal government passed Title IX of the Education Amendments, prohibiting discrimination on the basis of sex in educational settings. Public schools were required to offer sports teams for both girls and boys. Girls' participation in interscholastic athletics increased nationwide from 300,000 prior to Title IX to 2.25 million in the mid-1990s.[3]

The success of professional woman athletes has increased the prominence of females in sports. In the 1970s female tennis, gymnastics, and ice skating stars became celebrities. In recent years, American women's soccer champions, Olympic teams, and the WNBA have brought images of strong women athletes into America's living rooms. People are accustomed to seeing girls on athletic fields and many parents encourage their daughters to participate in sports. In fact, although many gender norms among teens have remained relatively stable over time, one important change has been an increase in girls' use of sports to gain social prestige.[4] By the 1990s female athletic participation had gained the attention of the Presidential Council on Physical Fitness and Sports, which published a report in 1997 summarizing research in the field.[5] Yet despite Title IX, federal money, and increased media attention, girls' athletic participation is still not equal to boys.[6] This is especially true for urban and poor youth. A recent study of a Canadian youth center found that despite high rates of participation in other organized activities, girls were still marginalized in the gym.[7]

Research indicates that some benefits of physical activity for adolescent girls go beyond the traditional health benefits associated with exercise. Female athletes are less likely to get pregnant, are more likely to postpone sexual intercourse, have fewer sexual partners, and are less likely to begin smoking cigarettes.[8] Sports have been found to reduce the chance of later adult diseases and to positively influence girls' motivation, self-perceptions, moral development, emotional well-being, stress, anxiety, and possibly self-esteem.[9] The President's Council on Physical Fitness and Sports asserted that physical activity is a developmental aid and public health asset for all youth.

Athletic opportunities may be particularly beneficial for the girls in urban after-school programs. African American and other ethnic minority girls tend to be less physically active than are Caucasian girls. Girls from economically disadvantaged neighborhoods also face greater barriers to regular physical activity and sports, including a lack of money for sports equipment or gym memberships and neighborhoods that may not provide safe environments for outdoor activity and exercise.[10] Yet athletic participation can be a social resource for minority youth.[11] Minority youth's athletic participation influences social involvement in school, community and extracurricular activities, and academic achievement.[12] Furthermore, because exercise reduces anxiety, it may be particularly beneficial for girls living in stressful environments,[13] such as high-poverty neighborhoods. Obesity is also on the rise in America, especially among children in urban areas; exercise is an important way to combat weight gain.[14]

In addition to being valuable to their health and development, sports and recreational activities provide enjoyment for the girls at these sites. As was seen in chapter 2, girls indicated in overwhelming numbers that physical activities were their favorite at the clubs. Given that the clubs have decades of experience with those activities, one might imagine, naively, that it would be a relatively simple matter to expand and improve physical recreational opportunities for girls. Yet it was not simple.

Before turning to our 3-year study of the East Side Club, let's look briefly at what we found during our first year of research in the four clubs that we studied at that time (we began our research at East Side in Year 2).

YEAR 1 OF THE GENDER EQUITY INITIATIVE: TENSIONS IN THE GYM

The gender equity initiative was an organization-wide attempt to improve the environment of the club for girls and to attract and retain more female members. The word *gender* referred in practice only to girls. The goals of the initiative centered on improving programs for girls. No mention was made of boys. This affected the evolution of the initiative in ways that were not foreseen by its architects.

One of the main goals of the initiative was to develop new girls' programs. Little emphasis, however, was given to sports programs for girls. Over time, we began to understand that the idea of girls' sports ran counter to what some staff members saw as traditional gender norms. During some of the gender sensitivity workshops, as the consulting psychologist presented our findings on the value that girls placed on sports at the clubs, some staff expressed fears about their girls becoming "too tough," stemming from their memories of rough girls from their own neighborhoods.[15] The prevailing assumption was that girls wanted to sit and chat with friends. Emphasis was placed on programs (such as Smart Girls) that highlighted group discussion and oftentimes were focused on developmental issues.

Girls often enjoyed these psychoeducational programs, but as the findings in chapter 2 make clear, even at the site with one of the best Smart Girls program, those girls indicated that double Dutch jump rope was their favorite activity. They wanted more physical activities and told us repeatedly of their frustrations over not having time to themselves in the gym. Although some girls participated in co-ed physical activities, other girls reported feeling as if they did not get a chance to play during co-ed time or not wanting to play with the boys. Furthermore, we observed girls relegated to the sidelines during time when both girls and boys were supposed to be on the floor. Among the teens nearly all the girls sat on the bleachers and watched the boys play.

For the boys, the prevailing opinion was that they couldn't be torn out of the gym. No thought was given to alternatives to sports, constraining boys' activity choices. A group of boys sitting around chatting did not fit with popular images of boys from these neighborhoods. Boys therefore had nothing better to do than to try to get the gym back from the girls.

Girls were frustrated, bored, and tired of having to fight for space. During co-ed time in the gym, boys had the upper hand. It was common to see girls sitting on the bleachers watching and talking rather than engaging in physical activity. When girls took initiative, lack of space or equipment often thwarted their efforts. There were few older teen girls in the clubs, and of those, few used the gym. There was little staff leadership for recreational activities that included older girls. The result was that only older girls who were self-motivated to seek out athletic opportunities used the gym. These were typically girls who had experience in sports and played on school teams. At some clubs there might also be one girl, around age 12 to 14, who played sports with the younger teen guys. For girls who tried to break the barriers, it took a fair amount of individual effort and persistence. Girls were often kept off of the court, passively or actively, and seldom were able to stand their ground successfully.

Many girls did not feel capable of such a struggle and were tired of having to continually battle for a ball or space on the court. Staff members tended to step in only when an open conflict occurred. We saw little proactive enforcement of gender equity in the gym. Many staff felt that they could not justify taking gym time away from the boys unless a critical mass of girls demanded their own gym time. Some staff and club directors reported that if teen girls showed up to use the gym they would allow them time to themselves in it. Yet the expectation of a spontaneous group of girls showing up to claim space in the gym was unrealistic given that there were only a handful of older teen girls at each club.

THE EAST SIDE CLUB: A 3-YEAR CASE STUDY

The East Side Club provides an opportunity for a detailed exploration of the issues faced in attempting to create a gender-equitable gym space. Such an in-depth analysis is important for a proper understanding of the practical challenges faced in making changes within an organization. A one-time-only snapshot of the issues involved in gender equity limits our abilities to apply the knowledge gained to other organizations and institutions. Understanding the evolution of the issues and the attempts to resolve them over time is key to identifying how other organizations can work toward gender equity and change.

We observed East Side over 3 years and through that time saw it grapple with problems, reach solutions, and attempt to maintain positive change in the face of adversity. Our first year at the East Side Club was the second year of the gender equity initiative, and thus we expected some strides would have already been made to address the issues posed by the initiative.

At the beginning of our first year at East Side, we met with the club directors to explain the research we would do. We alerted them that we would pay particular attention to the treatment of girls in the gym, as we had observed that this issue was a problem at other clubs. They assured us they had gone through the same struggles as the other clubs but that they had dealt with the issues and had no current problems. They had implemented once-a-week girls-only gym time years ago and said that it was now understood and the boys were okay with it, especially now that they had their own group that got them out of the gym and into other areas of the club. Given the directors' confidence, we expected to find a gym space that was used equally by boys and girls and that offered girls time to themselves without boys trying to take over. However, that is not what we found.

Our First Year at East Side

A three-person research team led by Nancy Deutsch began making site visits to East Side in the fall of the second year of the gender equity initiative. The researchers spent a lot of time in the gym, and sometimes all three had to be there to follow the action that was taking place, as well as to identify who was not in the gym and thus not helping out.

Cheryl was the staff person at East Side who led the effort to increase sports offerings for girls. Introduced in previous chapters, Cheryl is a 30ish woman with boundless energy and one of the world's biggest smiles. Cheryl started out at East Side working as a receptionist. Her enthusiasm and way with girls early on brought her to the attention of the director of the gender equity initiative. With the support of club leadership, Cheryl was promoted and encouraged to develop a variety of programs for girls.

The following detailed field note is a compilation of excerpts from the notes that three researchers made describing one evening in early autumn. It is representative of many of our visits to East Side during that first year, highlighting the enjoyment the girls found in physical activities as well as the tensions that existed between the girls and boys. By the end of the field note, it should be clear why we refer to interaction in the gym as gender wars.

We [the three researchers] *all go into the gym and sit down on the bleachers while* [the cheerleading team gets] *into their formation in the center of the gym floor.* [Fourteen girls ranging in age from 8 to 16 are on the floor. The three research assistants sit in the bleachers, watching the practice.] *A couple of the girls, who are new to the squad, sit on the bleachers with us . . . The girls on the floor are all dressed casually, in jeans and T-shirts . . . Cheryl comments as they arrange themselves, telling girls when they are out of place. Once they are in the correct places Cheryl tells them to begin. One girl starts them off by yelling a command and the girls start their cheer and movements. Cheryl stops them each time they do something incorrectly or aren't in sync. They then start again. "You're on a football field with thousands of people in the stands—no one is going to hear you!" she yells. The girls work their way through three cheers, starting over multiple times when Cheryl corrects them. When one girl starts to laugh, Cheryl stops them and says, "You got to be serious. You are performing." Rick* [the club director] *comes in and sits down at one point, watching. He smiles and makes some joking comments. "Good job!" he says at the end, clapping.* [Rick then leaves the gym.]

Cheryl then gets the girls to gather in the middle of the gym floor and begins to have them run laps, do jumping jacks, and do cartwheels. She does not let them rest and if someone doesn't do something she tells them to run two laps. The girls complain and roll their eyes and grumble and say they are tired but they all comply with Cheryl's instructions. The most they do in terms of not following her instructions is to occasionally cut the corners when they are running their laps . . . Three girls in particular have trouble staying focused. One is eating Skittles® from her pocket during practice and two keep giggling and talking to each other. Cheryl makes them run extra laps, which they do only when she is paying attention. When her back is turned towards them they slow down, sit on the ground, and giggle amongst each other. . . .

There are . . . a few boys and a few girls sitting on the bleachers watching throughout the practice. They come and go as they please. At one point, one of the boys who came in runs onto the court and Cheryl escorts him out all the way to the door but right after she turns around he comes right back in and sits on the bleachers . . . Another boy, about 11 or 12 years old, comes in and sits on the bleachers. He makes comments as he watches, saying "they can't do that," etc. Cheryl turns to him: "Don't be saying what my girls can't do. They couldn't even flip when they started and look at them now. Everyone has to learn, you weren't born flipping. So you keep your mouth shut about what they can't do." Later on he says something again and one of the girls, a very petite 12-year-old who, despite her small frame, has a tough demeanor and a stony look on her face, retorts to him, "Don't be telling me what I can't do.

Let's see you get out there and do that. Don't tell me I can't do it." She comes over to him and thrusts her chin out at him. The boy shrugs and goes onto the floor as Cheryl says, "Yeah, let's see what you can do." The boy attempts a cartwheel, to the catcalls of the girls as they say, "That's not a cartwheel! Look at your legs up there—what's all that!" Cheryl laughs. "With all your talk I expected you to come out here and be doing back flips and stuff!" The boy attempts a few more cartwheels and the girls imitate him and laugh. He is laughing too and continues to attempt cartwheels despite the laughter and pointing of the girls. The one girl who had told him that he couldn't tell her what she couldn't do attempts to coach him on how to do a cartwheel, telling him to stay on the line and demonstrating how his legs should go straight up and down not "all over like that."

. . . The last exercise Cheryl runs is a series of jumping jacks, which she makes the girls do in perfect unison. When they break the unison she has them start over, and every time someone complains she increases the number of jumping jacks they will have to perform. By the end she tells them that they will have to perform 140 jumping jacks, but she ends up letting them go before they are even close to that number. Tomorrow, she tells them, they will be doing Taebo.®

[After the cheerleading practice] . . . Cheryl announces that it is time for volleyball practice. She asks Shonda to put up the net . . . and I [researcher] go over to help her. As we are getting out the net . . . a couple of teen males come into the gym carrying a basketball. . . . As more young men come in they carry basketballs and begin running around the gym taking practice layups. Within about 15 minutes there are 10 or 12 young men in the gym. Cheryl, upon seeing that the boys are taking up the whole gym, begins yelling. "We got volleyball practice tonight," she cries. "Volleyball practice! You guys stay on half the gym because we got a game next Thursday and we got to practice!" The boys ignore her and Cheryl grows more upset. "Hey, y'all ask Charles [the male physical education director] if you don't believe me!" she says. The boys begin to notice her and as she continues to yell at them about eight of them cluster around her in a circle, effectively pinning her. Most of them are taller than she is and some of them are bumping and shoving her. . . . "We gotta practice. We got a game tomorrow," [the guys say]. Cheryl looks at them and says, "We've got half the gym for volleyball practice." "But we've got a game." "I don't care, so do we." The boys complain a little more but Cheryl stands her ground, speaking sternly and directly into their faces, although they are taller than her. She walks right up to them, only about two inches from their faces, and holds her head high looking them in the eyes, telling them that girls' volleyball practice has half the gym . . . She keeps yelling and finally storms out of the gym to find Charles. After she leaves, a young man holding a basketball emphatically shuts the gym door behind her . . . Cheryl comes back in with Charles but there is no need to regulate at this point as the boys seem to have resigned themselves to occupying only half the gym.

Once we [the girls and research assistants] have the net set up Cheryl asks Shonda to start a practice circle with the girls. We all form a circle and begin to practice bumping and tipping the ball around the circle. Cheryl has left

the gym. After a while the girls challenge us to a game, them versus us. Susie,
Erin, and I [the three researchers] go to one side of the net and the other six
girls . . . go to the other side. . . . We begin to play. After a couple of minutes
Cheryl returns and says, "This isn't fair!" and joins our side. We play three
games of volleyball, with our team winning all three. Cheryl gives pointers to
the girls as we play, and once actually stops and doesn't return a volley, al-
lowing them the point, because she is so proud of their play that she goes over
to the other side to high-five them all. She applauds them for good tries even if
their attempt isn't successful. While we are playing, the basketball game on the
other end of the court gets bigger, but there is no interaction between the guys
and the girls. Every now and then the volleyball is hit over onto the court and
the guys may say "Hey—watch your ball!" but it is always while smiling and
tossing the ball back . . . Charles joins them at some point

This episode demonstrates the rather mixed situation we found in our first year at the East Side club. The girls did have time to themselves in the gym, which they enjoyed. They actively engaged in a variety of physical activities, including volleyball and cheerleading. They learned skills and developed discipline. Cheryl encouraged and taught them.

Yet there was considerable conflict over ownership of the gym. Despite the directors' statements that the boys knew and respected the girls' time, the reality was that without Cheryl there to stand up for them, and her threat to get Charles, the girls had little hope of claiming the space. The directors' perceptions of the situation, that everything was fine, was markedly different from the reality of the situation as lived by Cheryl and the girls. Getting gym time for the girls required the presence of a staff member willing to stand her ground quite aggressively to keep the guys on half the court. And it was not until Cheryl left, promising to bring a male staff member back with her, that the boys acquiesced. Club leadership did not recognize that supporting girls' gym time when the girls or Cheryl asked for help was not the same as proactively protecting that time.

What is noticeable in this scenario is not only what did occur, but what did not. Imagine how the scene could have gone. While the cheerleaders were practicing, the doors to the gym could have been closed. No one would have been on the bleachers, which would have prevented the heckling. When the cheerleading practice finished, Charles could have been in the gym, helping the girls set up the volleyball net. He could have been there when the boys arrived and informed them himself that they would be playing half-court tonight. This would have eliminated the confrontation between Cheryl and the boys, which not only frustrated and angered her, but sent a clear message to the girls that they did not have equal rights to the gym in the boys' eyes.

The issue at East Side was not one of staff opposition to girls' gym time or of lack of leadership for girls' activities. What kept East Side from matching the rosy description of its directors was staff complacency. Whereas

Cheryl actively fought for girls' time in the gym, it was clear that if she were not there, the girls would not get the gym. Neither Cheryl nor the girls faulted club leadership or Charles for this. In fact, Cheryl spoke highly of Rick, the club director, and saw him as an advocate of her girls' programs (indeed, he made a point to stop by the gym and cheer them on early in the preceding episode). Charles, she said, was a great support to her and the girls. The girls expressed a fondness for Charles and saw him as someone who cared about and assisted them. Despite this, Cheryl was the only one who proactively defended the girls' right to physical activity. Charles backed her up, and Rick supported her programs, but she had to ask for help when she needed it. The girls, too, expressed an inability to claim space on their own and relied on Cheryl to fight for them. Thus, the girls' access to athletic activity was dependent on the strength of one staff person. This was a precarious situation. If Cheryl was sick or on vacation, or left the club, the girls were likely to lose their gym time. The proactive enforcement of girls' gym time at East Side was not what it should have been. This foreshadows problems to come.

Yet, East Side was ahead of other clubs in its provision of girls' recreational activities and gym time. The situation at the North River Club that same year was worse than that at East Side. Maria Pagano, the principal researcher at the North River Club, drew Figure 6.1 to illustrate the tension that she frequently observed between boys and girls in the gym. The boys, sure in their ownership of the space, do not notice or pay attention to the girls on the court. They are engaged in their game and having fun. The girls appear both frustrated and resigned. The girl on the left stands with a hand on her hip, the unused ball under her arm. Although obviously unhappy, she does not seem prepared to take an active stance against the boys. The girl on the right strikes a more defiant pose. Her crossed arms and irritated expression reveal her dissatisfaction with the situation. She appears more assertive than the other girl, but also is not taking action to rectify the situation. What is perhaps most telling about this picture is what is missing. No adult is present to help the girls break onto the court. There is no Cheryl at North River.

Without adults monitoring the gym, girls were left open to the possibility of harassment. Furthermore, because many of the girls in the clubs did not play sports, some felt self-conscious or simply uncomfortable playing in front of boys. Research indicates a greater drop in female participation in mixed-sex than in single-sex sports during adolescence. A common reason girls report for preferring single-sex sports is harassment and embarrassment at being watched. Girls say that boys laugh at them, put them down, and make rude comments during co-ed physical education classes.[16] Girls-only sports activities allow girls to play without the pressure of fitting into boys' playing styles or dealing with male-dominated games or attitudes.[17] Thus, girls-only time in the gym with oversight by adult staff was an important part of increasing physical opportunities for older girls.

Figure 6.1. The gym at the North River Club.

One reason for the lack of proactive involvement was that staff were accustomed to boys coming into the gym and playing pickup games of ball or shooting hoops on their own, with or without staff participation. However, in thinking that girls would begin to use the gym on their own, as the boys did, staff presumed a level of knowledge and skill that most of the girls did not have. Research indicates that girls are actually more interested than boys in beginning or increasing their level of athletic participation, yet report a lack of skills as a barrier.[18] Many of the girls at the clubs had never played organized sports and did not have the experience to start their own games. When staff or volunteers took the initiative to lead them in sports, girls responded with enthusiasm. The presence of adults who played with the girls increased their enjoyment of the gym and the probability of their using it.

Girls at North River, although they had time to themselves in the gym, were left on their own to both initiate activities and defend their space. Boys often came into the gym during girls' gym time and ignored the girls' protests and insistences that they leave. Staff were not generally in the gym and, if they wandered in during girls' gym time, did not always ask the boys to leave. The only person who consistently tried to defend the girls' rights to use the gym was the mother of a club member who came periodically and shot hoops with the girls. She took the initiative to begin basketball games, which the girls responded to and enjoyed. She also insisted that the staff get the boys out of the gym during girls' time and would go get staff if boys did enter the room. Yet even so, her efforts were often thwarted by a lack of proactive enforcement by club staff. For example, one evening she and one of our researchers began a basketball game with two teen girls. The game was interrupted by teen boys as soon as the mother left the gym to use the restroom. When the mother returned 5 minutes later she attempted to get the boys to leave the gym. The boys cursed at the woman and got up into her face. Although a staff member eventually intervened and made the boys leave the gym, he did not do so until after the mother had unsuccessfully attempted to get the boys to leave. The woman's confrontation with the boys left her visibly upset for the rest of the evening.

Our Second Year at East Side: Making Progress

The situation in the gym was transformed radically during our second year because of Cheryl's efforts. Although she herself was not especially athletic, she became the prime organizer of an inter-club girls' sports league that made a major impact on the club, as is evident in the following field note.

> I walked into the gym and found approximately 70–80 people sitting on the bleachers cheering and yelling and clapping. The people on the bleachers nearest the door were all youth I recognized from East Side. It was a mixture of boys and girls (about half and half) . . . A volleyball game was taking place on the floor of the gym. The net was set up across the gym horizontally and six girls (approximately 13–18, all African American) stood on each side of the net. On the side nearest the door was the East Side girls' volleyball team. They were all wearing red shorts with white T-shirts that had the logo of the girls' sports league on them. Janet and Cheryl [East Side coaches] both stood on the sidelines and were yelling encouragement, clapping, and providing tips about how to do things better. On the other side of the court was the New City Club's girls' team. . . . The girls appeared very serious about the game, and they would congratulate other girls on their team when they made a good play but would also chastise them if they didn't go for the ball or did something badly. Charles was standing on the end of the net farthest from the bleachers with a whistle in his mouth. He was the referee for the game and would blow his whistle and point to the team whose ball it was. Every now and then the New City team would make a face about one of his calls, but no one ever challenged him on his calls.
>
> When East Side won a point Jess would do a little dance. If one of the East Side girls made a bad play Cheryl would clap loudly and say, "That's okay, that's okay, good try, good try." The game was quite good, and the score was

close. There were a number of volleys and the more the ball went back and forth the louder the cheering got. Kids were pumping their fists in the air, yelling, clapping, stomping their feet on the bleachers, and jumping up and doing little dances when East Side won a point. . . .

. . . Sheila [a female staff member at East Side] came into the gym and stood next to me. She said hello and I said I was really impressed by the turnout for the game. She nodded. I asked who the people on the other bleachers were. "Oh, that's the New City basketball team. They brought them to support the girls. Our team is here too. The girls have always gone to the boys' games to support them and now the boys are coming to the girls' games." . . . The East Side team won and the kids from the bleachers jumped up, cheering and dancing and yelling. The majority of the kids ran down the bleachers and out onto the court, running up to the girls and hugging them and giving them high fives. Both boys and girls were dancing and hugging the girls' team.

Despite the initial neglect of girls' sports programs in the clubs, when Cheryl began an inter-club girls' sports league, the results were phenomenal. The league became the most successful new program for girls implemented during the gender equity initiative, involving a greater number of older girls than any other program. Clubs city-wide took part, expanding athletic opportunities for girls at numerous Boys & Girls Clubs. Furthermore, teen girls participated enthusiastically. Some girls who had stopped coming to the clubs returned just to play on the sports teams. Although the league began in our first year of observations at East Side, it took off in the second year. The results were apparent both at East Side individually and organization-wide.

The sports league involved clubs from across the city in a yearlong girls-only athletics program. Sports were rotated throughout the year, with a season each for softball, volleyball, and basketball. Many of the girls played on all of the teams and for most it was their first exposure to the various sports. Thus, the league provided two incentives to girls: specific athletic skills and social experiences. Girls interacted with others from their own club as well as from clubs around the city. This was a draw to the teens, who often talked about wanting more opportunities to meet youth from other clubs. Boys were drawn into the league through support of their respective girls' teams. The games thus provided a safe and fun environment for co-ed interactions among teens from different neighborhoods.

The inter-club aspect also led to organizational support for the league. Rick, the East Side Club director, came to the softball games, cooking hot dogs and hamburgers for the players. Girls' gym time became an organizational focus and the sports league provided clubs with a visible way to demonstrate that they were complying with the mandate to give girls gym time. Cheryl knew which clubs participated and the regional headquarters could use that as a measuring stick for girls' athletics programs. The institutional support for the league was important in conferring both resources and a sense of importance to the girls. As the girls' teams gained popularity, the boys became more supportive. Girls' gym time became less confrontational and more accepted.

In addition to inter-club tournaments, the league also fostered less dramatic but more regular physical activities for girls. The girls' sports teams had weekly practices led by Cheryl or Charles. These practices involved girls in skill-building exercises and pickup games. Practices were usually held during girls' gym time, allowing girls to develop their skills in a safe, un-self-conscious environment. When practices did occur during co-ed time, the fact that the girls were part of an organized team conferred greater legitimacy to their need for half the gym.

East Side also drew on other youth as resources. Cheryl had older girls assist with practices which helped keep them in the club. This also capitalized on the diversity of girls' motives for sports participation. Other studies have found that girls talked about cooperation, support, and teaching younger children as important aspects of their involvement in an organized sports team.[19] In addition, the boys' basketball team sometimes scrimmaged with the girls' team. These games, supervised by Cheryl and Charles, garnered enthusiasm among the teens and allowed girls to practice their skills during friendly, co-ed competition.

The girls' sports league was successful not only for what it provided the girls but also for what it opened up to the boys. The boys were exposed to a number of new sports. Some of the boys were interested in the sports they saw, and this motivated staff to start new activities for boys in addition to the usual basketball, football, and floor hockey.

Despite the inarguable success of the sports league, it provided opportunities only for girls who wanted to play competitive sports. Girls who preferred informal physical activity—who just wanted to toss the ball around occasionally—still had nothing to do. This posed its own barrier to girls' gym use. Research suggests that girls are often motivated to play sports by factors such as the opportunity for having fun, fitness, and social bonds, including making new friends.[20] It was important to provide opportunities centered on the social and fitness aspects of physical activity in addition to team sports.

Such programs, when developed, were successful. In addition to the sports teams, East Side began a dance group. This was a very popular activity and drew girls who may not have been engaged by team sports. Cheryl had boys and girls come together to develop dance routines for club talent shows and events. During rehearsals, there was lots of activity and laughter and boys and girls both danced enthusiastically and expressed excitement over new ideas for moves. Cheryl would stand on the sidelines, clapping her hands and stomping her feet to the music, providing encouragement but allowing the youth to develop their own ideas and choose their own music. Girls tended to do most of the choreography, developing steps in pairs and then teaching them to the group. They danced in boy–girl pairs, with a few girl–girl pairs when there were not enough boys. In this manner, Cheryl drew both boys and girls into dance as an alternative physical activity in which girls took on leadership roles. This capitalized on the teenagers' love of music and dance and desire for co-ed interaction. It also expanded the activities available and provided both boys and girls with a noncompetitive form of physical activity.

A second positive development during this year was the expansion of a boys' group led by Charles. (Chap. 4 includes a discussion of this program, which was popular with the teen boys at East Side.) The boys openly talked to Charles about topics as personal as wet dreams. This was facilitated by Charles' own self-disclosure about potentially embarrassing subjects and his creative use of popular culture to initiate discussion about sensitive topics. The boys at East Side frequently mentioned Charles's group as an example of their positive experiences at the club. They clearly appreciated Charles's attention and talked about how he taught them to be responsible men. In addition to providing the boys with support for developmental areas often ignored in male adolescents, the all-male discussion group also made girls' gym time seem less like a loss. The boys now had their own group and their own time in which to talk candidly among themselves. This kept them from hanging around waiting at the gym doors, a problem that we observed in Year 2 at both East Side and North River.

In combination, the girls' sports league and the development of the boys' group made the gym a less contentious space. Things now worked more easily for girls in the gym. The gender wars had dissipated at the East Side Club.

Our Third Year at East Side: An Uncertain Future

The story of the gender equity initiative is one of ups and downs, even at East Side. The most successful clubs put a lot of time and energy into girls' sports. Often, this was the pet project of one staff person. At the East Side Club, Cheryl was devoted to girls' programming and spent an extraordinary amount of time and energy organizing the sports league and other activities and events for girls. Although she reported receiving support from club leadership, the programs still relied on her to run them. When she received a promotion and was given more extensive duties, the girls' programs began to languish. Cheryl began to have older girls coach the sports teams, as she no longer had the time to do so. Although this was a creative solution to the immediate problem, it did not address the long-term issue that girls' programming was overly reliant on a single staff member.

At the beginning of our third year at East Side, both Cheryl and Charles left the club. Although Charles returned to the club later in the year, what happened in the aftermath of their departures is illustrative of one of the major issues faced by the clubs. These two staff members ran the only gender-oriented programs for older youth at the club. The popularity of the staff was a major draw for teens. Their absence left a hole not only in the programming of the club, but in the social support networks of the youth as well.

When Cheryl left the East Side Club, the girls' sports program ended, at least temporarily. Although new staff were hired, they had different interests. After her departure, teenage girls began to complain that there was nothing to do at the club. Throughout the fall and winter, normally the big seasons for the sports league, there were no girls' sports. A new staff person began a dance program which was popular with the older youth and younger teens but did not fill the gap for the girls who had played on the sports teams. By early winter most of the older girls had disappeared from the club.

The mother of one of the girls who played on the volleyball team spear-headed an effort to restart the sports programs, and in the spring organized a mother–daughter volleyball tournament. When Charles returned to the club in the spring he took over coaching the girls' softball team, which would play in the inter-club league over the summer. It is not clear, however, whether the girls sports league would continue on the scale that it was when Cheryl was at the club. Furthermore, more than six months passed in which the girls had no sports activities, and the effect was clear in the girls' attendance.

The all-boys group also disbanded when Charles left. The older boys, who had always come to the club to play basketball, appeared to dwindle in number. Despite the stereotype that the boys wanted nothing more than to play basketball it seems that Charles was part of the draw for them. When Charles returned, so did the boys. Although the discussion group did not begin again immediately, the rumor was that it would, and the boys spoke of that possibility with hope.

CONCLUSION

Over the 4 years that we were in the Boys & Girls Clubs, we saw administrators and staff take steps toward the goals of the gender equity initiative. In particular, we saw the gym, center stage for the tension between boys and girls at the club, evolve into a less all-male sphere. Although this evolution is not complete and differs widely between clubs, strides have been made in many clubs toward making the gym an environment that welcomes girls and boys equally. The success of the transformations, however, rests on a number of factors, and it remains to be seen how many of these will be maintained over time.

One important, and recurring, underlying problem was faulty assumptions made regarding gender differences. The initial assumption that girls would be drawn more to discussion groups than to sports, and that boys were interested only in more basketball and would disdain reflective opportunities, turned out to be deeply flawed. Girls overwhelmingly indicated that physical activities were their favorite, and boys flocked to discussion groups when offered by popular staff. A focus on stereotypical gender differences constrained opportunities for both girls and boys.

However, in a Shakespearean-like comedy of errors, at times the clubs assumed there would not be gender differences, when in fact gender differences were quite important. In particular, it was assumed that girls' participation style in the gym would be like that of the boys. Instead, girls needed active staff leadership. Moreover, a number of girls sought gym time only for tossing the ball around with friends and did not care for competitive sports.

True gender equity must highlight both the areas of overlap and the areas of difference. It must recognize divergence, but not at the expense of similitude. The question should not be sameness versus difference, but sameness and difference. Gender refers to both boys and girls. Ways need to be found to provide equal opportunities that move beyond assumptions and stereotypes and are responsive to both the similarities and differences in developmental experiences.

CHANGING THE CULTURE
OF THE CLUB

A strategy that seeks gender equity by addressing only girls places the burden of equity on the shoulders of girls without asking any changes of boys, staff, or the culture of the organization more broadly. Girls cannot be focused on in isolation. Actions taken to increase opportunities for girls will affect the boys. It will lead to less gym time for boys and they will not like that. They especially will not like it when they are not given anything else very interesting to do. As boys in the clubs saw more and more new programs developed for girls, they demanded more of those for themselves as well. And, contrary to deeply ingrained stereotypes, the boys participated with enthusiasm in new programs when offered by popular staff. Gender does not and should not refer to girls only. Boys need to be offered a wider array of programs to provide space for the girls' as well as for the boys' development.

Changes in staff behavior and the culture of the setting are needed as well. This should not be surprising given the history of the setting. These were, after all, boys clubs until fairly recently. The gender equity initiative sought to realize more fully the potential of the sites as a place for boys *and* girls. Yet the importance of the gym in the overall culture of the site was not adequately addressed. Changing the culture involved more than changing the gym, but the culture of the gym was a core element of these after-school sites.

The clubs are very successful in creating a positive culture when they put their mind to it. They have clear rules against fighting, cursing, and wearing hats or gang colors. These are clearly and repeatedly detailed to youth in a very public manner. Violators are subject to disciplinary action, including suspension. We know that this effort has been successful because we repeatedly heard youth enforce the rules among themselves when staff were not present.

But culture creation has not as yet been extended to the treatment of girls in the gym. As was noted repeatedly in this chapter, staff do not pro-actively support girls' use of the gym in a manner that addresses girls' needs. They do not easily provide leadership for informal physical activities. They do not publicly and repeatedly inform boys of rules that require respecting girls' use of the gym. Although some clubs have signs or posters that present positive views of girls or encourage their participation, there is typically no such signage in the gym.

Creating a sustainable culture means that gender equity needs to be a shared responsibility. It cannot be on the shoulders of a single staff person. It needs to be addressed proactively and comprehensively by all.

NOTES

1. See Hirsch et al. (2000) for an early report on aspects of the gender equity initiative.
2. President's Council on Physical Fitness and Sports (1997).
3. President's Council on Physical Fitness and Sports (1997).
4. Suitor & Reavis (1995).
5. President's Council on Physical Fitness and Sports (1997).
6. President's Council on Physical Fitness and Sports (1997).
7. Wilson, White, & Fisher (2001).
8. Aaron, Dearwater, Anderson, Olsen, Kriska, & Laporte (1995); Sabo, Miller, Farrell, Barnes, & Melnick (1998); Sabo, Miller, Farrell, Milnick, & Barnes (1999).
9. Delaney & Lee (1995); President's Council on Physical Fitness and Sports (1997).
10. President's Council on Physical Fitness and Sports (1997).
11. Melnick, Sabo, & Vanfossen (1992).
12. Acosta (1993).
13. President's Council on Physical Fitness and Sports (1997).
14. President's Council on Physical Fitness and Sports (1997).
15. Le Menestrel et al. (2002) note that girls still suffer from the tomboy stigma.
16. Engel (1994).

17. Wilson et al. (2001).

18. Varpalotai & Doherty (2000).

19. Wilson et al. (2001).

20. Ryckman & Hamel (1992); Varpalotai & Doherty (2000); Weinberg, Tenenbaum, McKenzie, Jackson, Anshel, Grove, et al. (2000).

III

CONCLUSION

7

BUILDING A BETTER
SECOND HOME

The most important finding of this research is that the relationships between youth and staff are the heart and soul, the most fundamental strength, of these urban after-school programs. The idea that these relationships are important is not new. Yet little prior research had examined them in any depth. Both our qualitative and quantitative results converge to suggest that, if anything, these relationships are even more powerful than had been thought. The assertion that youth–staff ties are the most fundamental strength implies that other features of these settings are not as fundamental. The main competitor in this regard is structured programming, but our findings indicate that the quality of implementation is too deficient. Better use could be made of structured programs, and I recommend how to do this later in the chapter, but they did not prove to be a core strength. Recreational activities are also important, but these activities do not appear to have as much developmental potential as mentoring and it proved difficult to consistently provide quality activities in a gender-equitable manner.

Because the importance of the youth–staff tie is the most communicable bottomline message of the book, I focus the first part of this chapter on that issue, rather than review results on several topics. I conclude the chapter by providing an overview of the agenda needed for after-school centers at this time. I hope that keeping the concluding chapter brief and focused maximizes the potential impact of the book on program development and social policy. I begin by summarizing relevant findings on the staff–youth relationship across chapters.

An initial finding that pointed toward the importance of youth–staff relationships came from our investigation into how these after-school sites might serve as second homes for youth. The fact that three fourths of youth reported that their club served as a second home is a testament to the important place of the club in their lives. The primary reason that the club was experienced as a second home was the quality of relationships at the club, rather than the physical characteristics of the site. Ties to adult staff were key in this regard.

The distinctive strengths of youth–staff relationships emerged especially clearly when we compared those ties with the relationships that youth reported with their closest adult kin and closest school-based adult. Whereas school adults mentored almost exclusively around academic issues, and kin mentored almost exclusively around nonacademic issues, club staff had a healthy balance of both. Club staff were the adults who most consistently helped youth with their homework; they also spent considerable time addressing a host of nonschool issues. Moreover, staff were noted for the positive way in which they framed their communication, consistent with a youth development rather than a deficit orientation.

The quantitative comparison of the linkage between each of these three youth–adult relationships with youth self-esteem provided further evidence of the distinct value of the youth–staff tie. The linkage to self-esteem was twice as powerful for the youth–staff as compared with the youth–kin tie, and more than four times as powerful as the youth–school tie. These analyses revealed that relationships with staff were especially important to youth who lived in the most violent neighborhoods.

A detailed examination of one staff member, Charles, demonstrated the impressive quality of mentoring at these sites. Charles fearlessly addressed a wide range of highly sensitive topics with the young guys at his club, provided guided introduction to cultures beyond the housing project, and displayed his affinity with his young charges through both word and deed.

Even when we turned to investigate the implementation of structured psychoeducational programs, the data reminded us of the importance of youth's relationship to staff. What youth remembered most positively was the great relationship they had with the adult leader, rather than any of the formal program elements.

The quality of youth–staff relationships, moreover, compares quite well with effective mentoring relationships as determined by a recent review of formal mentoring programs.[1] The exceptionally large amount of time spent together, the willingness to have fun as well as educate, and the involvement of staff with youth's family and friends are consistent with best practices.

The fact that ties to staff were of equal value to boys and girls is another finding well worth noting. Research on ties to extended family members had typically found girls reporting stronger ties than did boys.[2] But in this study, there were no gender differences in either the absolute amount of support received from staff or the linkage of support and self-esteem.[3] Eleanor Maccoby argued that gender differences are most likely to occur when stereotypical behavior is demanded by same-gender peer groups.[4] However, it is clear that staff such as Charles are highly esteemed and sought after by teen boys. And Charles role-models being both hard and soft in ways that cut through gender stereotypes. So the social environment of the club encourages young boys to develop close ties to adult staff.

The ability of club staff to connect effectively to adolescent boys, mentoring them, bolstering and protecting their self-esteem, finding acceptable alternatives to violence, is something that should be of great interest to policymakers and funders. Adolescent boys in low-income urban communities are at high risk for dropping out of school, winding up in prison, or being murdered. And they are notoriously hard to reach. It is hard to get and keep them in programs that can make a difference. These after-school sites have found a way to engage many of them and to provide them with helpful mentors. This is no small accomplishment.

This type of after-school program thus provides what I have referred to as one-stop shopping for mentoring. Staff help young people develop their skills, make positive choices, and cope with the myriad stressors of early adolescence and urban life. They do this for boys as well as girls and in some ways they provide a wider range of mentoring than does any other nonparental adult in these youngsters' lives.

After-school programs with strong youth–staff relationships draw on and, in important ways, replicate positive features of the youth's familial environment and peer group. They provide a bridge between the youth's natural social environment and the outside world, creating similar processes that function first to engage and then socialize youth to positive identities. Staff make adaptive use of this shared cultural affinity to develop exceptionally wide-ranging mentoring relationships. When combined with formal psychoeducational programs, these processes provide a synergy for promoting youth development that makes these settings unique.

If mentoring is a core strength of comprehensive urban after-school sites, then how can programs build on this strength? What are potential obstacles and problems and how can they best be addressed?

A STRATEGY FOR IMPROVEMENT

The value we found in mentoring relationships across clubs provides a model for what could be offered at every club. There is considerable potential, yet not all of that potential is being realized. Some staff are ambivalent about the role of mentor. Some need to develop additional skills. Some believe that they don't have enough time to spend on mentoring. Some don't know how to extend the range of their mentoring. To fully develop the mentoring potential at each site, more organizational leadership and structure is needed, as well as greater support at the policy level.

Leadership

Studies of change in educational settings have made it clear that the role of the organizational leader is critical to making change work.[5] It is no different at these after-school sites. Program directors need to make staff mentoring a core feature of the organizational culture. Six steps are needed to support this objective.

First, the role of mentoring needs to be clearly articulated as a part of the leader's vision for the program. The leader needs a vision, it needs to be expressed, and mentoring should be at its core.

Second, the program director, or someone else in a leadership position, needs to provide ongoing training and supervision in the development of mentoring relationships. Club staff typically bring strong interpersonal skills, but they can often use guidance in how to use these in the service of mentoring youth. Even among those highly skilled, there is always room for professional growth. Indeed, development of skills can help sustain excitement in the work over time. Training and supervision should be provided in both staff conferences and one-to-one formats.

Third, staff should mentor youth in as many ways as possible to develop positive identities. The different facets discussed in chapter 4 provide a framework for assessing and directing staff efforts. These elements include

- fostering youth initiative;
- socializing youth to specific positive identities;
- providing opportunities for youth skill development;
- providing helpful feedback to youth;
- providing emotional support;
- promoting codeswitching;
- serving as positive role models; and
- socializing peer friendship groups.

Fourth, program leaders need to appreciate that staff need downtime to spend with youth. Hanging out with youth and joking around with them can help the relationship to develop and provide emotional glue. Sometimes staff are doing plenty when they appear to be doing nothing. Of course, that is not always true, and effective leaders need to know and appreciate the difference.

Fifth, given the importance of relationships, programs need to be especially sensitive to how staff departures can affect youth. The sites we studied tended not to give sufficient time for youth to grieve over the lost or soon-to-be-lost relationship. More attention and time need to be devoted to the termination process. This is one area where consultation with those with experience and expertise is probably needed. Program leaders in particular need to separate their own responses, especially if they terminated the employee for cause, from what would help the youth at their setting.

Sixth, success stories need to be celebrated. Everyone needs to feel that he or she is effective. Success stories can provide emotional support to staff to keep them going over time, as well as provide clues as to how the best mentoring can be accomplished.

Structure

Relationships emerge from shared activities. Structured program activities can provide a mechanism for developing stronger relationships between youth and staff. Well-designed activities can promote more rigorous learning and skill development, providing opportunities for staff to support youth identities at a more demanding level. In addition, as we saw for both Charles and Aurelia, structured formats can lead staff to address a wider range of issues, and in greater depth, than they would do in the absence of such programs.

At the same time, structured programs have the potential to diminish the quality of interpersonal relationships. Youth can feel that marching through required activities is more important than getting to know and appreciate them as individuals. Researchers from Public/Private Ventures, for example, make a considerable effort to argue that it is important to have fun with mentees and not just spend all the time together focusing on academics.[6] Too much focus on what youth need to learn can easily turn into a deficit orientation, which is not what young people need or expect in these settings.

Another problem facing highly structured programs is their lack of fit with the culture of these settings. Although there is variability, many of these settings do not have a great deal of structure. Attempts to implement rigid programs are not likely to succeed in such an environment.

Thus, it is important to fashion a way to introduce a greater level of structured programming that will work at these sites. The new structure must add to rather than subtract from the quality of the youth–staff relationships, and fit rather than cause friction with club culture.

More realistic benchmarks for determining how much content should be covered in a session would make it much easier to do both structure and process well. The guidelines for several Smart Girls sessions greatly overestimated how much material girls at that age could actually make use of and retain. Only so much emotionally laden material can be handled at any one time. If the objective is to have real-world impact on youth, rather than just being able to mark off lots of covered material on a checklist, then the emphasis should be on the quality rather than the quantity of material covered. These types of programs often seem driven by curriculum developers attempting to cram facts into young heads, and can easily lose sight of the forest by attending too much to individual trees. The goals for any session should be few in number and represent a distillation of the bottomline objectives.

Many tactics can be used to attain a session's overarching objectives. In particular, communication styles that emphasize step-by-step logic should not be privileged over folk ways of relating, such as in Charles' use of the rhetorical strategies of vernacular African American English. There are lots of ways to get a point across and after-school programs are places where, in contrast to schools, greater flexibility is possible and should be encouraged. If nonstandard English helps staff connect with youth and become more effective mentors, then staff should draw on that as a resource.

The greater danger here is that if too much content is provided, then staff may wind up feeling compelled to follow what appears to be a prescribed format. Yet if structure is seen as an aid to process, then staff leaders should be encouraged to use their own style and expertise in presenting the suggested content. In general, effective staff in these settings seem to enjoy and make good use of self-disclosure and storytelling. They draw on their own experience and personalize the material. This sharing of self is part of what draws youth to staff and makes them role models. Programs should find a way to augment this process. Program material should encourage and facilitate such efforts.

Some evaluation findings suggest the potential value of proceeding in this direction. Botkin, Schinke, and colleagues, for example, found that a narrative, storytelling approach to prevention was significantly superior to the standard curricular approach to information provision and skill development among minority early adolescents.[7] More such programs need to be developed and evaluated.

This more relational, process-oriented approach differs significantly from the classroom orientation that reflects the roots of many program developers, including university researchers. I am familiar with this way of teaching and can personally testify to its drawbacks. From my own experience teaching college students, I know that there are times when if I let a good discussion proceed, I will not get to talk about facts or perspectives that I had hoped to address. However, too much detail can kill a discussion. So I have to make a choice. In classroom and classroom-like settings, the choice tends to be in favor of content coverage. However, to promote relationships, to realize the distinct potential of after-school sites, the choice should be in favor of keeping the discussion going and keeping youth engaged in ways that make sense to them. Less detail may be covered, but the overarching objectives can still be addressed without disturbing the dynamics of the relationship and diminishing its quality.

Program developers should forge hands-on collaborations with expert staff such as Charles in developing programs in this new format. The collaboration should be with frontline staff, rather than those who have moved up to administrative roles and, often, lost touch with the day-to-day realities of working with youth and implementing programs. The emphasis in program development should explicitly be on program effectiveness, on what is likely to be implemented well and be effective with youth in garden-variety after-school settings, rather than on designing ideal curricula that at best will work (be efficacious) only under highly supported conditions that rarely if ever occur in the real world. Both program developers and frontline staff such as Charles can contribute their expertise so that the design process supports and augments the natural mentoring that occurs.

This approach can help introduce more structure and improve the quality of after-school programs, without diminishing the interpersonal processes that result in rich youth–staff ties. Indeed, the fundamental orientation becomes how structure can enhance relationships. In seeking structure that complements process, this strategy draws on rather than fights against the culture of the setting. It appreciates and draws on the strengths of the setting while challenging it to rise to new levels of excellence. This approach should increase the prospects for successful implementation and for sustaining programs over time.

Policy

I have argued in this book that comprehensive, urban after-school programs with strong staff mentors provide crucial supports to low-income youth and that they are well worth supporting. Here, I would like to emphasize some specific policies that would help these centers recruit and retain their most important resource: high quality staff.

One of the main problems vexing after-school centers is high staff turnover. The greater the benefits delivered by high-quality youth–staff relationships, the greater the cost of turnover in achieving program objectives. Staff at after-school centers are rarely well paid and, clearly, their salaries should be increased. Similarly, staff should be provided a standard benefit package, including health insurance.

Many staff take college courses part-time. Mostly these are taken at the undergraduate level, but one or two take master's-level courses and more might if the financial burden were eased. The federal or state government could subsidize educational loans for youth workers. This subsidy could be in the form of lower interest rates and forgiveness of portions of the loan contingent on future employment in the youth field.

The purpose of this research was to generate a better understanding of the nature and value of this type of urban after-school program. The type is characterized by comprehensive activities and strong interpersonal relationships. The strength of the relationships is reflected both in ties among youth and in ties to adult staff. The ability of these programs to provide high-quality, wide-ranging mentoring is perhaps their greatest asset from a developmental and policy perspective.

The existence of strong interpersonal ties in the programs we studied provides a marked contrast to findings from the evaluation of the 21st Century Community Learning Centers.[8] The evaluation found that the Centers had a negligible effect on academic and psychosocial variables. The academic activities were not very rigorous and often amounted to study halls. For those concerned with improving academic performance, these results may argue for more focused academic skill training. And some of that may well be useful, especially for youth who are doing poorly in school. However, our findings suggest that the failure of the Centers to generate an engaging peer climate and to promote strong youth–staff relationships may also be a critical factor accounting for their lack of effectiveness. Stronger academic programs may be needed, but stronger relationships are important as well.[9] It would be shortsighted and mistaken to believe that a tight focus on academics alone is the way to go. Relationships and having fun with friends help to attract and retain youth in these settings. And strong staff mentors may contribute to academic motivation and performance. Beyond school, staff help youth develop the range of knowledge, values, and skills that youth need to become good citizens and productive members of society.

Broadly conceived, these programs seem to nicely complement the attention of kin to nonacademic issues, and the focus of schools on academic concerns. Indeed, one of the most important developmental assets of these sites is their ability to support an integrated set of evolving, positive identities and to bridge familial and nonfamilial worlds. This ability is key in thinking of the array of supports that need to be provided to urban adolescents.

The fact that these programs are well received by so many early adolescents should not be taken for granted. Prior efforts to design schools especially for this age group—first the junior high, then middle schools—do not provide much of a success story. The repeated shortcomings of these schools might lead one to question whether it is even possible to create satisfactory environments for this age group. Given this history, the positive response of youth to the after-school programs we studied, particularly in crime-ridden low income neighborhoods, is a remarkable accomplishment and a strong argument against tampering with them in any fundamental way. In the search for better designs for after-school programs, policy makers should not throw out the baby with the bathwater. Comprehensive after-school programs with strong staff mentoring relationships need to be maintained.

At the same time, there is little reason to be complacent. Staff need to improve their mentoring skills, programs need to be more rigorous and challenging, and basic recreational opportunities need to be provided equitably to girls and boys. Comprehensive after-school programs need to improve.

This type of urban after-school program has not been the subject of as much scholarly attention as have highly structured academic or psychosocial programs. In particular, although youth–staff relationships have typically been considered to be a central resource, there has been little in-depth qualitative research and no statistical analyses of quantitative data on these ties. Nor had prior studies of these settings provided much in the way of theory to explain results. I hope that the convergence of our qualitative and quantitative findings, and the linking of our findings to theory and empirical work in other domains, has added to the study's richness and potential importance and opened up new lines of inquiry for future researchers. Although I believe that this investigation makes a contribution to the field, it is by no means the final word. The field needs more in-depth studies of relationship processes, structured activities of all kinds, and linkages with parents and schools, as well as longitudinal follow-ups to determine impacts. In short, a lot more research on comprehensive after-school programs is needed.

Keep, improve, and study the programs—a tall but manageable agenda for our times.

NOTES

1. See meta-analysis by DuBois et al. (2002).
2. Hirsch et al. (2002).
3. A number of other investigators have also found that overlap among boys and girls can be substantial. Way (1998), for example, in a study of friendships among urban high school students, found a similar interest across gender in having close friendship. Youniss and Smollar (1985) found that only one third of boys demonstrated a substantially weaker pattern of friendship than did girls in adolescence.
4. Maccoby (1998).
5. Fullan (1991); Sarason (1982).
6. Herrera et al. (2000).
7. Botvin, Schinke, Epstein, Diaz, & Botvin (1995).
8. Dynarski et al. (2003).
9. See Schinke et al. (2000) for a study of the effectiveness of enhanced academic programs at Boys & Girls Clubs.

REFERENCES

Aaron, D., Dearwater, S., Anderson, R., Olsen, T., Kriska, A., & Laporte, R. (1995). Physical activity and the initiation of high-risk health behaviors in adolescents. *Medicine and Science in Sports & Exercise, 27*, 1639–1645.

Acosta, R. (1993). The minority experience in sport: Monochromatic or Technicolor? In G. L. Cohen (Ed.), *Women in sport: Issues and controversies* (pp. 204–213). Newbury Park, CA: Sage.

Allen, J., Kuperminc, G., Philliber, S., & Herre, K. (1994). Programmatic prevention of adolescent problem behaviors: The role of autonomy, relatedness, and volunteer services in the Teen Outreach Program. *American Journal of Community Psychology, 22*, 617–638.

Anderson, E. (1989). Sex codes and family life among poor inner-city youths. *Annals of the American Academy of Political and Social Science, 501*, 59–78.

Anderson, E. (1990). *Streetwise: Race, class, and change in an urban community.* Chicago: University of Chicago Press.

Anderson, E. (1999). *Code of the street: Decency, violence, and the moral life of the inner city.* New York: Norton.

Arbreton, A., & McClanahan, W. (2002). *Targeted outreach: Boys & Girls Clubs of America's approach to gang prevention and intervention.* Philadelphia: Public/Private Ventures.

Asante, M. (1998). *The afrocentric idea* (Rev. & expanded ed.). Philadelphia: Temple University Press.

Aschenbrenner, J. (1978). *Lifelines: Black families in Chicago.* New York: Holt, Rinehart & Winston.

Baker, K., Pollack, M., & Kohn, I. (1995). Violence prevention through informal socialization: An evaluation of the South Baltimore Youth Center. *Studies on Crime and Crime Prevention, 4*, 61–85.

Baldwin, J. (1895). *Mental development of the child and the race: Methods and processes.* New York: Macmillan.

Bandura, A. (1986). *Social foundations of thought and action: A social cognitive theory.* Englewood Cliffs, NJ: Prentice Hall.

Baumrind, D. (1991). Parenting styles and adolescent development. In R. Lerner, A. Petersen, & J. Brooks-Gunn (Eds.), *Encyclopedia of adolescence* (pp. 746–757). New York: Garland.

Belle, D. (1999). *The after-school lives of children: Alone and with others while parents work.* Mahwah, NJ: Erlbaum.

Benson, P. (1997). *All kids are our kids: What communities must do to raise caring and responsible children and adolescents.* San Francisco: Jossey-Bass.

Berman, P. (1980). Thinking about programmed and adaptive implementation: Matching strategies to situations. In H. Ingram & D. Mann (Eds.), *Why policies succeed or fail* (pp. 205–227). Thousand Oaks, CA: Sage.

Berman, P., & McLaughlin, M. (1978). *Federal programs supporting educational change: Vol. 8. Implementing and sustaining innovations.* Washington, DC: U.S. Office of Education.

Blakely, C., Menon, R., & Jones, D. (1995). *Project BELONG: Final report.* College Station: Texas A&M University, Public Policy Research Institute.

Blumenstein, A. (2000, May). Factors contributing to the ups and downs of youth violence. In W. J. Wilson (Chair), *Youth violence in urban communities.* Conference presented at Kennedy School of Government, Harvard University, Cambridge, MA.

Boorman, G. D., Hewes, G., Overman, L. T., & Brown, S. (2002). *Comprehensive school reform and student achievement: A meta-analysis.* CRESPAR Report #59. Baltimore: Johns Hopkins University, Center for Research on the Education of Students Placed At Risk.

Botvin, G., Schinke, S., Epstein, J., Diaz, T., & Botvin, E. (1995). Effectiveness of culturally focused and generic skills training approaches to alcohol and drug abuse prevention among minority adolescents: Two-year follow-up results. *Psychology of Addictive Behaviors, 9,* 183–194.

Boys & Girls Clubs of America. (1997). *SMART Girls manual.* Atlanta, GA: Boys & Girls Clubs of America.

Branch, C. W. (1999). Pathologizing normality or normalizing pathology? In C. W. Branch (Ed.), *Adolescent gangs: Old issues, new approaches* (pp. 197–211). Philadelphia: Brunner/Mazel.

Brehm, J., & Gates, S. (1997). *Working, shirking, and sabotage: Bureaucratic response to a democratic public.* Ann Arbor: University of Michigan Press.

Brown, C. (1999). The role of school when school is out. *The Future of Children, 9,* 139–143.

Brunswick, A. F., & Rier, D. A. (1995). Structural strain: Drug use among African American youth. In R. L. Taylor (Ed.), *African-American youth: Their social and economic status in the United States* (pp. 225–246). Westport, CT: Praeger.

Buka, S., Stichick, T., Birdthistle, I., & Earls, F. (2000, May). The epidemiology of witnessing community violence in childhood and adolescence. In W. J. Wilson (Chair), *Youth violence in urban communities.* Conference presented at Kennedy School of Government, Harvard University, Cambridge, MA.

Bukowski, W., Newcomb, A., & Hartup, W. (Eds.). (1996). *The company they keep: Friendships in childhood and adolescence.* New York: Cambridge University Press.

Burton, L. M., Allison, K. W., & Obeidallah, D. (1995). Social context and adolescence: Perspectives on development among inner-city African-American teens. In L. J. Crockett & A. C. Crouter (Eds.), *Pathways through adolescence: Individual development in relation to social contexts* (pp. 119–138). Mahwah, NJ: Erlbaum.

Call, K., & Mortimer, J. (2001). *Arenas of comfort in adolescence: A study of adjustment in context.* Mahwah, NJ: Erlbaum.

Campbell, A. (1991). *The girls in the gang* (2nd ed). Cambridge, MA: Basil Blackwell.

Canada, G. (1995). *Fist Stick Knife Gun*. Boston: Beacon Press.

Cantwell, N. (1992). The origins, development and significance of the United Nations Convention on the Rights of the Child. In S. Detrick (Ed.), *The United Nations Convention on the Rights of the Child: A guide to the travaux préparatoires* (pp. 19–30). Boston: Martinus Nijhoff.

Carnegie Corporation of New York. (1992). *A matter of time: Risk and opportunity in the nonschool hours*. New York: Self.

Catalano, R., Berglund, M., Ryan, J., Lonczak, H., & Hawkins, J. (1999). *Positive youth development in the United States: Research findings on evaluations of positive youth development programs*. Seattle: Social Development Research Group, University of Washington School of Social Work.

Chaiken, M. (1998). Tailoring established after-school programs to meet urban realities. In D. Elliott, B. Hamburg, & K. Williams (Eds.), *Violence in American schools: A new perspective* (pp. 348–375). New York: Cambridge University Press.

Charles Stewart Mott Foundation. (1998). *Press release: Poll finds overwhelming support for after-school enrichment programs to keep kids safe and smart*. Flint, MI: Author.

Chase-Lansdale, P. L., Moffitt, R. A., Lohman, B. J., Cherlin, A. J., Coley, R. L., Pittman, L. D., et al. (2003, March 7). Mothers' transitions from welfare to work and the well-being of preschoolers and adolescents. *Science, 299,* 1548–1552.

Chawla, L. (1992). Childhood place attachments. In I. Altman & S. M. Low (Eds.), *Place attachment: Vol. 12. Human behavior and environment: Advances in theory and research* (pp. 63–86). New York: Plenum Press.

Cho, H. (1995). Children in the examination war in South Korea: A cultural analysis. In S. Stephens (Ed.), *Children and the politics of culture* (pp. 141–168). Princeton, NJ: Princeton University Press.

Cicchetti, D., & Lynch, M. (1993). Toward an ecological/transactional model of community violence and child maltreatment: Consequences for children's development. *Psychiatry, 56,* 96–118.

Clark, C. M. (1992). Deviant adolescent subcultures: Assessment strategies and clinical interventions. *Adolescence, 27,* 283–293.

Cole, T. (1999). Ebbing epidemic: Youth homicide rate at a 14-year low. *Journal of the American Medical Association, 281,* 25–26.

Coleman, J. (1961). *The adolescent society*. New York: Free Press.

Collins, P. H. (1991). *Black feminist thought: Knowledge, consciousness, and the politics of empowerment*. New York: Routledge.

Connell, J., Gambone, M., & Smith, T. (2000). *Youth development in community settings: Challenges to our field and our approach*. Philadelphia: Public/Private Ventures.

Cooley, C. (1902). *Human nature and the social order*. New York: Charles Scribner's Sons.

Corsaro, W. (1997). *The sociology of childhood*. Thousand Oaks, CA: Pine Forge Press.

Cotterell, J. L. (1991). The emergence of adolescent territories in a large urban leisure environment. *Journal of Environmental Psychology, 11*, 25–41.

Cotterell, J. L. (1993). Do macro-level changes in the leisure environment alter leisure constraints on adolescent girls? *Journal of Environmental Psychology, 13*, 125–136.

Cotterell, J. L. (1996). *Social networks and social influences in adolescence*. New York: Routledge.

Cowie, H. (1999). Peers helping peers: Interventions, initiatives, and insights. *Journal of Adolescence, 22*, 433–436.

Cross, W., Jr., & Strauss, L. (1998). The everyday functions of African American identity. In J. Swim & C. Stangor (Eds.), *Prejudice: The target's perspective* (pp. 267–279). San Diego, CA: Academic Press.

Cuban, L. (1992). What happens to reforms that last? The case of the junior high school. *American Educational Research Journal, 29*, 227–251.

Damon, W. (1995). *Greater expectations: Overcoming the culture of indulgence in America's homes and schools*. New York: Free Press.

Dane, A., & Schneider, B. (1998). Program integrity in primary and early secondary prevention: Are implementation effects out of control? *Clinical Psychology Review, 18*, 23–45.

Delaney, W., & Lee, C. (1995). Self-esteem and sex roles among male and female high school students: Their relationship to physical activity. *Australian Psychologist, 30*, 84–87.

Detrick, S. (Ed.). (1992). *The United Nations Convention on the Rights of the Child: A guide to the "travaux préparatoires."* Boston: Martinus Nijhoff.

Domitrovich, C., & Greenberg, M. (2000). The study of implementation: Current findings from effective programs that prevent mental disorders in school-aged children. *Journal of Educational and Psychological Consultation, 11*, 193–221.

Douvan, E., & Adelson, J. (1966). *The adolescent experience*. New York: Wiley.

DuBois, D., Holloway, B., Valentine, J., & Cooper, H. (2002). Effectiveness of mentoring programs for youth: A meta-analytic review. *American Journal of Community Psychology, 30*, 157–197.

DuBois, D., & Neville, H. (1997). Youth mentoring: Investigation of relationship characteristics and perceived benefits. *American Journal of Community Psychology, 25*, 227–234.

DuBois, D., Neville, H., Parra, G., & Pugh-Lilly, A. (2002). Testing a new model of youth mentoring. In J. Rhodes (Ed.), *A critical view of youth mentoring* (pp. 21–57). San Francisco: Jossey-Bass.

Duncan, G., & Chase-Lansdale, P. L. (2001). Welfare reform and child well-being. In R. Blank & R. Haskins (Eds.), *The new world of welfare* (pp. 391–417). Washington, DC: Brookings Institution Press.

Durlak, J. (1997). *Successful prevention programs for children and adolescents*. New York: Plenum.

Durlak, J. (1998). Why program implementation is important. *Journal of Prevention & Intervention in the Community, 17*, 5–18.

Durlak, J., & Wells, A. (1997). Primary prevention mental health programs for children and adolescents. *American Journal of Community Psychology, 25*, 115–152.

Durlak, J., & Wells, A. (1998). Evaluation of indicated preventive intervention (secondary prevention) mental health programs for children and adolescents. *American Journal of Community Psychology, 26*, 775–802.

Dynarski, M., Pistorino, C., Moore, M., Silva, T., Mullens, J., Deke, J., et al. (2003). *When schools stay open late: The national evaluation of the 21st-Century Community Learning Centers program*. Washington, DC: U.S. Department of Education.

Eccles, J., Midgley, C., Wigfield, A., Buchanan, C., Reuman, D., Flanagan, C., et al. (1993). Development during adolescence: The impact of stage-environment fit on young adolescents' experiences in schools and in families. *American Psychologist, 48*, 90–101.

Elias, M. (1997). Reinterpreting dissemination of prevention programs as widespread implementation with effectiveness and fidelity. In R. Weissberg, T. Gullotta, R. Hampton, B. Ryan, & G. Adams (Eds.), *Healthy Children 2010: Establishing preventive services* (pp. 253–289). Thousand Oaks, CA: Sage Publications.

Elmore, R. (1978). Organizational models of social program implementation. *Public Policy, 26*, 185–228.

Elmore, R. (1982). Backward mapping: Implementation research and policy decisions. In W. Williams (Ed.), *Studying implementation: Methodological and administrative issues* (pp. 18–35). Chatham, NJ: Chatham House.

Engel, A. (1994). II. Sex roles and gender stereotyping in young women's participation in sport. *Feminism & Psychology, 4*, 439–448.

Erikson, E. (1968). *Identity: Youth and crisis*. New York: Norton.

Ervin, L. H., & Stryker, S. (2001). Theorizing the relationship between self-esteem and identity. In S. Stryker, T. J. Owens, & N. Goodman. (Eds.), *Extending self-esteem theory and research: Sociological and psychological currents* (pp. 29–55). New York: Cambridge University Press.

Fagan, J., & Wilkinson, D. (1998). Social contexts and functions of adolescent violence. In D. Elliott, B. Hamburg, & K. Williams (Eds.), *Violence in American schools: A new perspective* (pp. 94–126). New York: Cambridge University Press.

Fashola, O. (2002). *Building effective afterschool programs*. Thousand Oaks, CA: Corwin Press.

Feldman, R., & Stall, S. (1994). The politics of space appropriation: A case study of women's struggles for homeplace in Chicago public housing. In I. Altman & A. Churchman (Eds.), *Women and the environment: Vol. 13. Human behavior and environment: Advances in theory and research* (pp. 167–199). New York: Plenum Press.

Ferguson, R. (1994). How professionals in community-based programs perceive and respond to the needs of black male youth. In R. Mincy (Ed.), *Nurturing black males* (pp. 59–98). Washington, DC: Urban Institute Press.

Field, N. (1995). The child as laborer and consumer: The disappearance of childhood in contemporary Japan. In S. Stephens (Ed.), *Children and the politics of culture* (pp. 51–78). Princeton, NJ: Princeton University Press.

Fine, G., & Mechling, J. (1993). Child saving and children's cultures at century's end. In S. B. Heath & M. W. McLaughlin (Eds.), *Identity and inner-city youth: Beyond ethnicity and gender* (pp. 120–146). New York: Teachers College Press.

Fine, G., & Sandstrom, K. (1988). *Knowing children: Participant observation with minors*. Thousand Oaks, CA: Sage.

Flannery, D. J., Huff, C. R., & Manos, M. (1998). Youth gangs: A developmental prospective. In T. P. Gullotta, G. R. Adams, & R. Montemayor (Eds.), *Delinquent violent youth: Theory and interventions: Vol. 9. Advances in adolescent development: An annual book series* (pp. 175–204). Thousand Oaks, CA: Sage.

Flynn, C. (1999). *On being twelve: The worlds of early adolescents in an urban neighborhood*. Unpublished doctoral dissertation, Northwestern University, Evanston, IL.

Fordham, S., & Ogbu, J. (1986). Black students' school success: Coping with the "burden of acting White." *The Urban Review, 18*, 176–206.

Frank, J. D. (1973). *Persuasion and healing: A comparative study of psychotherapy* (2nd ed.). Baltimore: Johns Hopkins University Press.

Frank, J. D., & Frank, J. B. (1991). *Persuasion and healing: A comparative study of psychotherapy* (3rd ed.). Baltimore: Johns Hopkins University Press.

Franklin, B. (Ed.). (1995). *The handbook of children's rights: Comparative policy and practice*. New York: Routledge.

Franklin, J. (1988). A historical note on black families. In H. P. McAdoo (Ed.), *Black families* (2nd ed., pp. 23–26). Newbury Park, CA: Sage.

Freedman, M. (1993). *The kindness of strangers*. San Francisco: Jossey-Bass.

Freeman, M., & Veerman, P. (Eds.). (1992). *The ideologies of children's rights*. Boston: Martinus Nijhoff.

Fullan, M. (1991). *The new meaning of educational change* (2nd ed.). New York: Teachers College Press.

Gambone, M., & Arbreton, A. (1997). *Safe havens: The contributions of youth organizations to healthy adolescent development*. Philadelphia: Public/Private Ventures.

Garbarino, J., Kostelny, K., & Dubrow, N. (1991). *No place to be a child: Growing up in a war zone*. Lexington, MA: Lexington Books.

Gee, J. P. (1996). *Social linguistics and literacies: Ideology in discourses* (2nd ed.). London: Taylor & Francis.

Gottfredson, D. (2001). *Schools and delinquency*. New York: Cambridge University Press.

Gottfredson, D., Fink, C., Skroban, S., & Gottfredson, G. (1997). Making prevention work. In R. Weissberg, T. Gullotta, R. Hampton, B. Ryan, & G. Adams

(Eds.), *Healthy Children 2010: Establishing preventive services* (pp. 219–252). Thousand Oaks, CA: Sage.

Gottfredson, D., Gottfredson, G., & Skroban, S. (1998). Can prevention work where it is needed most? *Evaluation Review, 22*, 315–340.

Greenberg, M., Domitrovich, C., & Bumbarger, B. (1999). *Preventing mental disorders in school-age children: A review of the effectiveness of prevention programs.* University Park: Pennsylvania State University, Prevention Research Center.

Grossman, J., & Johnson, A. (1999). Assessing the effectiveness of mentoring programs. In J. Grossman (Ed.), *Contemporary issues in mentoring* (pp. 48–65). Philadelphia: Public/Private Ventures.

Grossman, J., Price, M., Fellerath, V., Juvocy, L., Kutloff, L., Raley, R., et al. (2002). *Multiple choices of after school: Findings from the extended-service initiative.* Philadelphia: Public/Private Ventures.

Grossman, J., & Rhodes, J. (2002). Length of mentoring relationship as a predictor of adolescent outcomes. *American Journal of Community Psychology, 30*, 199–220.

Grossman, J., & Tierney, J. (1998). Does mentoring work: An impact study of the Big Brothers Big Sisters program. *Evaluation Review, 22*, 403–426.

Grotevant, H. (1998). Adolescent development in family contexts. In N. Eisenberg (Ed.), *Handbook of child psychology: Vol. 3. Social, emotional, and personality development* (5th ed., pp. 1097–1149). New York: Wiley.

Gutman, H. (1976). *The black family in slavery and freedom, 1750–1925.* New York: Random House.

Halpern, R. (1992). The role of after-school programs in the lives of inner-city children: A study of the "Urban Youth Network." *Child Welfare, 71*, 215–230.

Halpern, R. (1999). After-school programs for low-income children: Promise and challenges. *Future of Children, 9*, 81–95.

Halpern, R. (2003). *Making play work: The promise of after-school programs for low-income children.* New York: Teachers College Press.

Halpern, R., Barker, G., & Mollard, W. (2000). Youth programs as alternative spaces to be: A study of neighborhood youth programs in Chicago's West Town. *Youth & Society, 31*, 469–506.

Hamilton, S., & Hamilton, M. (1992, March). Mentoring programs: Promise and paradox. *Phi Delta Kappan*, pp. 546–550.

Harter, S. (1990). Self and identity development. In S. Feldman & G. Elliott (Eds.), *At the threshold: The developing adolescent* (pp. 352–387). Cambridge, MA: Harvard University Press.

Harter, S. (1999). *The construction of the self: A developmental perspective.* New York: Guilford.

Harter, S., Bresnick, S., Bouchey, H. A., & Whitesell, N. R. (1997). The development of multiple role-related selves during adolescence. *Development and Psychopathology, 9*, 835–853.

Hawkins, J. D., Catalano, R., & Associates. (1992). *Communities that care: Action for drug abuse*. San Francisco: Jossey-Bass.

Heath, S. B., & McLaughlin, M. W. (1993). Ethnicity and gender in theory and practice: The youth perspective. In S. B. Heath & M. W. McLaughlin (Eds.), *Identity and inner-city youth: Beyond ethnicity and gender* (pp. 13–35). New York: Teachers College Press.

Hegel, G. W. F. (1977). *Phenomenology of spirit* (A. V. Miller, Trans.). New York: Oxford University Press. (Original work published 1807)

Herrera, C., Sipe, C., & McClanahan, W. (2000). *Mentoring school-age children: Relationship development in community-based and school-based programs*. Philadelphia: Public/Private Ventures.

Heymann, J. (2000). *The widening gap: Why America's working families are in jeopardy and what can be done about it*. New York: Basic.

Hirsch, B. J. (1980). Natural support systems and coping with major life changes. *American Journal of Community Psychology, 8*, 159–172.

Hirsch, B. J. (1981). Social networks and the coping process: Creating personal communities. In B. Gottleib (Ed.), *Social networks and social support* (pp. 149–170). Beverly Hills, CA: Sage.

Hirsch, B. J., & DuBois, D. (1992). The relation of peer social support and psychological symptomatology during the transition to junior high school: A two-year longitudinal analysis. *American Journal of Community Psychology, 20*, 333–347.

Hirsch, B. J., & Jolly, E. A. (1984). Role transitions and social networks: Social support for multiple roles. In V. L. Allen & E. van de Vliert (Eds.), *Role transitions: Explorations and explanations* (pp. 39–51). New York: Plenum.

Hirsch, B. J., Mickus, M., & Boerger, R. (2002). Ties to influential adults among black and white adolescents: Culture, social class, and family networks. *American Journal of Community Psychology, 30*, 289–303.

Hirsch, B. J., & Rapkin, B. (1987). The transition to junior high school: A longitudinal study of self-esteem, psychological symptomatology, school life, and social support. *Child Development, 58*, 1235–1243.

Hirsch, B. J., Roffman, J., Deutsch, N., Flynn, C., Loder, T., & Pagano, M. (2000). Inner city youth development organizations: Strengthening programs for adolescent girls. *Journal of Early Adolescence, 20*, 210–230.

hooks, b. (1990). *Yearning: Race, gender, & cultural politics*. Boston: South End Press.

Hubble, M., Duncan, B., & Miller, S. (Eds.). (1999). *The heart and soul of change: What works in therapy*. Washington, DC: American Psychological Association.

Huff, C. R. (1990). *Gangs in America*. Newbury Park, CA: Sage.

Institute of Medicine, Committee on Prevention of Mental Disorders. (1994). *Reducing risks for mental disorders: Frontiers for preventive intervention research* (P. Mrazek & R. Haggerty, Eds.). Washington, DC: National Academy Press.

James, A., Jenks, C., & Prout, A. (1998). *Theorizing childhood*. Cambridge, England: Polity Press.

James, A., & Prout, A. (Eds.). (1997). *Constructing and reconstructing childhood: Contemporary issues in the sociological study of childhood* (2nd ed.). London: Falmer Press.

James, W. (1890). *Principles of psychology*. Chicago: Encyclopedia Britannica.

Johnson, A., & Sullivan, J. (1995). Mentoring program practices and effectiveness. In M. Galbraith & N. Cohen (Eds.), *Mentoring: New strategies and challenges* (pp. 43–56). San Francisco: Jossey-Bass.

Kaltreider, D., & St. Pierre, T. (1995). Beyond the schools: Strategies for implementing successful drug prevention programs in community youth-serving organizations. *Journal of Drug Education, 25*, 223–237.

Kaplan, A. (1964). *The conduct of inquiry*. San Francisco: Chandler.

Kohut, H. (1977). *The restoration of the self*. New York: International Universities Press.

Kohut, H. (1984). *How does analysis cure?* Chicago: University of Chicago Press.

Korpela, K. M. (1989). Place-identity as a product of environmental self-regulation. *Journal of Environmental Psychology, 9*, 241–256.

Korpela, K. M. (1992). Adolescents' favorite places and environmental self-regulation. *Journal of Environmental Psychology, 12*, 249–258.

Korpela, K. M., & Hartig, T. (1996). Restorative qualities of favorite places. *Journal of Environmental Psychology, 16*, 221–233.

Kotlowitz, A. (1991). *There are no children here: The story of two boys growing up in the other America*. New York: Anchor.

Lambert, M. (1992). Implications of outcome research for psychotherapy integration. In J. Norcross & M. Goldfried (Eds.), *Handbook of psychotherapy integration* (pp. 94–129). New York: Basic Books.

Lareau, A. (2000). Social class and the daily lives of children: A study from the United States. *Childhood, 7*, 155–171.

Larson, R. (2000). Toward a psychology of positive youth development. *American Psychologist, 55*, 170–183.

Larson, R., Richards, M. H., Sims, B., & Dworkin, J. (2001). How urban African American young adolescents spend their time: Time budgets for locations, activities, and companionship. *American Journal of Community Psychology, 29*, 565–597.

LeBlanc, L. (1995). *The Convention on the Rights of the Child: United Nations lawmaking on human rights*. Lincoln: University of Nebraska Press.

Le Menestrel, S., Bruno, M., & Christian, D. (2002). *Sports as a hook: An exploratory study of developmentally focused youth sports programs*. Washington, DC: Academy for Educational Development.

Lerner, R. (1995). *America's youth in crisis: Challenges and options for programs and policies*. Thousand Oaks, CA: Sage.

Lester, J., Bowman, A., Goggin, M., & O'Toole, L. (1987). Public policy implementation: Evolution of the field and agenda for future research. *Policy Studies Review, 7*, 200–216.

Limber, S., & Wilcox, B. (1996). Application of the UN Convention on the Rights of the Child to the United States. *American Psychologist, 51,* 1246–1250.

Linder, S., & Peters, B. (1987). A design perspective on policy implementation: The fallacies of misplaced prescription. *Policy Studies Review, 6,* 459–475.

Lipsitz, J. (1984). *Successful schools for young adolescents.* New Brunswick, NJ: Transaction Books.

Little, J., & Wynn, J. (1989). *The availability and use of community resources for young adolescents in an inner-city and a suburban community.* Chicago: Chapin Hall Center for Children, University of Chicago.

Loder, T., & Hirsch, B. (2003). Inner city youth development organizations: The salience of peer ties among early adolescent girls. *Applied Developmental Science, 7,* 2–12.

Low, S. M., & Altman, I. (1992). Place attachment: A conceptual inquiry. In I. Altman & S. M. Low (Eds.), *Place attachment: Vol. 12. Human behavior and environment: Advances in theory and research* (pp. 1–12). New York: Plenum Press.

Maccoby, E. (1998). *The two sexes: Growing up apart, coming together.* Cambridge, MA: Harvard University Press.

Maccoby, E., & Martin, J. (1983). Socialization in the context of the family: Parent-child interaction. In P. H. Mussen (Series Ed.) & E. M Hetherington (Vol. Ed.), *Handbook of child psychology: Vol. 4. Socialization, personality, and social development* (4th ed., pp. 1–101). New York: Wiley.

Mahoney, J., Stattin, H., & Magnusson, D. (2001). Youth recreation centre participation and criminal offending: A 20-year longitudinal study of Swedish boys. *International Journal of Behavioral Development, 25,* 509–520.

Majors, R., & Billson, J. (1992). *Cool pose: The dilemmas of black manhood in America.* New York: Simon & Schuster.

Mandara, J. (in press). The impact of family functioning on African American males' academic achievement: A review and clarification of the empirical literature. *Teachers College Record.*

Marcus, C. C. (1992). Environmental memories. In I. Altman & S. M. Low (Eds.), *Place attachment: Vol. 12. Human behavior and environment: Advances in theory and research* (pp. 87–112). New York: Plenum Press.

Markus, H., & Nurius, P. (1986). Possible selves. *American Psychologist, 41,* 954–969.

Martin, E., & Martin, J. M. (1978). *The black extended family.* Chicago: University of Chicago Press.

Maslow, A. (1968). *Toward a psychology of being* (2nd ed.). New York: Van Nostrand.

Matland, R. (1995). Synthesizing the implementation literature: The ambiguity-conflict model of policy implementation. *Journal of Public Administration Research and Theory, 5,* 145–174.

McKeon, R. (Ed.). (1941). *The basic works of Aristotle.* New York: Random House.

McLaughlin, M. (1991). Learning from experience: Lessons from policy implementation. In A. Odden (Ed.), *Education policy implementation* (pp. 185–195).
Albany, NY: SUNY Press.

McLaughlin, M. W. (1993). Embedded identities: Enabling balance in urban contexts. In S. B. Heath & M. W. McLaughlin (Eds.), *Identity and inner-city youth:
Beyond ethnicity and gender* (pp. 36–67). New York: Teachers College Press.

McLaughlin, M., Irby, M., & Langman, J. (1994). *Urban sanctuaries: Neighborhood
organizations in the lives and futures of inner city youth.* San Francisco: Jossey-
Bass.

McLearn, K., Colasanto, D., & Schoen, C. (1998). *Mentoring makes a difference:
Findings from The Commonwealth Fund 1998 Survey of Adults Mentoring Young
People.* New York: The Commonwealth Fund.

McLoyd, V. (1998). Children in poverty: Development, public policy, and practice.
In I. Sigel & K. Renninger (Eds.), *Handbook of child psychology: Vol. 4. Child
psychology in practice* (5th ed., pp. 135–208). New York: Wiley.

Mead, G. (1934). *Mind, self, and society from the standpoint of a social behaviorist.*
Chicago: University of Chicago Press.

Melnick, M., Sabo, D., & Vanfossen, B. (1992). Educational effects of interscholastic athletic participation on African-American and Hispanic youth. *Adolescence, 27*, 295–308.

Melton, G. (1991). Socialization in the global community: Respect for the dignity
of children. *American Psychologist, 46*, 66–71.

Metropolitan Life. (1994). *Metropolitan Life Survey of the American teacher. Violence
in America's public schools: A survey of students, teachers, and law enforcement officers.* Alexandria, VA: National Association of Elementary School Principals.

Moos, R. (1976). *The human context: Environmental determinants of behavior.* New
York: Wiley.

Morrow, K., & Styles, M. (1995). *Building relationships with youth in program settings:
A study of Big Brothers/Big Sisters.* Philadelphia: Public/Private Ventures.

Musick, J. (1993). *Young, poor, and pregnant: The psychology of teenage motherhood.*
New Haven, CT: Yale University Press.

National Research Council and Institute of Medicine (NRC/IOM) Committee on
Community-Level Programs for Youth. (2002). *Community programs to promote
youth development* (J. Eccles & J. Gootman, Eds.). Washington, DC: National
Academy Press.

Newman, K. (1996). Working poor: Low-wage employment in the lives of Harlem
youth. In J. Graber, J. Brooks-Gunn, & A. Petersen (Eds.), *Transitions through
adolescence: Interpersonal domains and contexts* (pp. 323–343). Mahwah, NJ:
Erlbaum.

Noam, G., & Miller, B. (Eds.). (2002). *Youth development and after-school time: A tale
of many cities.* San Francisco: Jossey-Bass.

O'Toole, L., Jr. (1986). Policy recommendations for multi-actor implementation:
An assessment of the field. *Journal of Public Policy, 6*, 181–210.

Overstreet, S., Dempsey, M., Graham, D., & Moely, B. (1999). Availability of family support as a moderate of exposure to violence. *Journal of Clinical Child Psychology, 28,* 36–45.

Owens, T. (1994). Two dimensions of self-esteem: Reciprocal effects of positive self-worth and self-deprecation on adolescent problems. *American Sociological Review, 59,* 391–407.

Pagano, M. (2000). *Non-parental social support and the well-being of low-income, minority youth.* Unpublished doctoral dissertation, Northwestern University, Evanston, IL.

Paikoff, R., & Brooks-Gunn, J. (1991). Do parent-child relationships change during puberty? *Psychological Bulletin, 110,* 47–66.

Palumbo, D., & Calista, D. (Eds.). (1990). *Implementation and the policy process: Opening up the black box.* New York: Greenwood Press.

Pastor, J., McCormick, J., & Fine, M. (1996). Makin' homes: An urban girl thing. In B. Leadbeater & N. Way (Eds.), *Urban girls: Resisting stereotypes, creating identities* (pp. 15–34). New York: New York University Press.

Peterson, L., & Rigby, K. (1999). Countering bullying at an Australian secondary school with students as helpers. *Journal of Adolescence, 22,* 482–492.

Phelan, P., Davidson, A., & Cao, H. (1991). Students' multiple worlds: Negotiating the boundaries of family, peer, and school cultures. *Anthropology & Education Quarterly, 22,* 224–250.

Phelan, P., Davidson, A., & Yu, H. C. (1997). *Adolescents' worlds: Negotiating family, peers, and school.* New York: Teachers College Press.

Pianta, R. (1999). *Enhancing relationships between children and teachers.* Washington, DC: American Psychological Association.

Pittman, K., Irby, M., & Ferber, T. (2000). *Unfinished business: Further reflections on a decade of promoting youth development.* Philadelphia: Public/Private Ventures.

Pittman, K., & Wright, M. (1991). *A rationale for enhancing the role of the non-school voluntary sector in youth development.* Washington, DC: Center for Youth Development and Policy Research.

President's Council on Physical Fitness and Sports. (1997). *Physical activity & sport in the lives of young girls: Physical & mental health dimensions from an interdisciplinary approach.* Washington, DC: U.S. Department of Health and Human Services.

President's Science Advisory Committee, Panel on Youth. (1974). *Youth: Transition to adulthood.* Chicago: University of Chicago Press.

Proshansky, H. M., Fabian, A. K., & Kaminoff, R. D. (1983). Place identity: Physical world socialization of the self. *Journal of Environmental Psychology, 3,* 57–83.

Quinn, J. (1999). Where need meets opportunity: Youth development programs for early teens. *The Future of Children, 9,* 96–116.

Qvortrup, J., Bardy, M., Sgritta, G., & Wintersberger, H. (Eds.). (1994). *Childhood matters: Social theory, practice and politics.* Brookfield, VT: Ashgate Publishing.

Rapoport, A. (1985). Thinking about home environments: A conceptual framework. In I. Altman & S. M. Low (Eds.), *Home environments: Vol. 8. Human behavior and environment: Advances in theory and research* (pp. 255–286). New York: Plenum Press.

Reiss, S. (1989). *City games*. Urbana: University of Illinois Press.

Relph, E. (1976). *Place and placelessness*. London: Pion Limited.

Rhodes, J. (2002). *Stand by me: The risks and rewards of mentoring today's youth*. Cambridge, MA: Harvard University Press.

Rhodes, J., Contreras, J., & Mangelsdorf, S. (1994). Natural mentor relationships among Latina adolescent mothers. *American Journal of Community Psychology, 22,* 211–228.

Richters, J., & Martinez, P. (1993). Violent communities, family choices, and children's chances: An algorithm for improving the odds. *Development and Psychopathology, 5,* 609–627.

Robertson, R. (1997). Walking the talk: Organizational modeling and commitment to youth and staff development. *Child Welfare, 76,* 577–589.

Roffman, J. (2000). *Non-parent support figures in the lives of inner-city youth*. Unpublished doctoral dissertation, Northwestern University, Evanston, IL.

Rogoff, B. (1990). *Apprenticeship in thinking: Cognitive development in social context.* New York: Oxford University Press.

Roth, J., Brooks-Gunn, J., Murray, L., & Foster, W. (1998). Promoting healthy adolescents: Synthesis of youth development program evaluations. *Journal of Research on Adolescence, 8,* 423–459.

Rubinstein, R. L., & Parmelee, P. A. (1992). Attachment to place and the representation of the life course by the elderly. In I. Altman & S. M. Low (Eds.), *Place attachment: Vol. 12. Human behavior and environment: Advances in theory and research* (pp. 139–163). New York: Plenum Press.

Ryckman, R., & Hamel, J. (1992). Female adolescents' motives related to involvement in organized team sports. *International Journal of Sports Psychology, 23,* 147–160.

Sabatier, P. (1986). Top-down and bottom-up approaches to implementation research: A critical analysis and suggested synthesis. *Journal of Public Policy, 6,* 21–48.

Sabo, D., Miller, K., Farrell, M., Barnes, G., & Melnick, M. (1998). *The Women's Sports Foundation report: Sport and teen pregnancy*. East Meadow, NY: Women's Sports Foundation.

Sabo, D., Miller, K., Farrell, M., Melnick, M., & Barnes, G. (1999). High school athletic participation, sexual behavior and adolescent pregnancy: A regional study. *Journal of Adolescent Health, 25,* 207–216.

Salmivalli, C. (1999). Participant role approach to school bullying: Implications for interventions. *Journal of Adolescence, 22,* 453–459.

Sarason, S. (1982). *The culture of the school and the problem of change* (2nd ed.). Boston: Allyn & Bacon.

Sartre, J.-P. (1966). *Being and nothingness: An essay on phenomenological ontology* (H. Barnes, Trans.). New York: Washington Square Press.

Savin-Williams, R., & Berndt, T. (1990). Friendship and peer relations. In S. Feldman & G. Elliott (Eds.), *At the threshold: The developing adolescent* (pp. 277–307). Cambridge, MA: Harvard University Press.

Schinke, S., Cole, K., & Poulin, S. (2000). Enhancing the educational achievement of at-risk youth. *Prevention Science, 1,* 51–60.

Schinke, S., Orlandi, M., & Cole, K. (1992). Boys & Girls clubs in public housing developments: Prevention services for youth at risk. *Journal of Community Psychology, 28,* 118–128.

Schorr, L. (1989). *Within our reach: Breaking the cycle of disadvantage.* New York: Doubleday.

Schubiner, H., Scott, R., & Tzelepis, A. (1993). Exposure to violence among inner-city youth. *Journal of Adolescent Health, 14,* 214–219.

Seidman, E. (in press). *Risky school transitions: An opportunity for educational reform.* Cambridge, MA: Harvard University Press.

Shimkin, D., Shimklin, E., & Frate, D. (Eds.). (1978). *The extended family in black societies.* Chicago: Aldine.

Simmons, R., & Blyth, D. (1987). *Moving into adolescence: The impact of pubertal change and school context.* New York: Aldine de Gruyter.

Sipe, C. (1996). *Mentoring: A synthesis of P/PV's research: 1988–1995.* Philadelphia: Public/Private Ventures.

Smitherman, G. (1977). *Talkin and testifyin: The language of Black America.* Boston: Houghton Mifflin.

Spencer, M., Cunningham, M., & Swanson, D. (1995). Identity as coping: Adolescent African-American males' adaptive responses to high-risk environments. In H. Harris, H. Blue, & E. Griffith (Eds.), *Racial and ethnic identity: Psychological development and creative expression* (pp. 31–52). New York: Routledge.

Stack, C. (1974). *All our kin: Strategies for survival in the black community.* New York: Harper & Row.

Stack, C. (1996). *Call to home: African Americans reclaim the rural south.* New York: Basic.

Staples, R., & Johnson, L. (1993). *Black families at the crossroads: Challenges and prospects.* San Francisco: Jossey-Bass.

Steinberg, L. (1990). Autonomy, conflict, and harmony in the family relationship. In S. Feldman & G. Elliott (Eds.), *At the threshold: The developing adolescent* (pp. 255–276). Cambridge, MA: Harvard University Press.

Stephens, S. (Ed.). (1995). *Children and the politics of culture.* Princeton, NJ: Princeton University Press.

Strozier, C. (2001). *Heinz Kohut: The making of a psychoanalyst.* New York: Farrar, Straus, & Giroux.

Stryker, S. (1980). *Symbolic interactionism: A social structural version.* Menlo Park, CA: Benjamin/Cummings Publishing.

Sudarkasa, N. (1988). Interpreting the African heritage in Afro-American family organization. In H. P. McAdoo (Ed.), *Black families* (2nd ed., pp. 27–43). Newbury Park, CA: Sage.

Suitor, J., & Reavis, R. (1995). Football, fast cars, and cheerleading: Adolescent gender norms, 1978–1989. *Adolescence, 30*, 265–272.

Taylor, R. (1996). Adolescents' perceptions of kinship support and family management practices: Association with adolescent adjustment in African American families. *Developmental Psychology, 32*, 687–695.

Taylor, R., & Roberts, D. (1995). Kinship support and maternal and adolescent well-being in economically disadvantaged African American families. *Child Development, 66*, 1585–1597.

Thoits, P. (1990). Social support and psychological well-being: Theoretical possibilities. In I. Sarason & B. Sarason (Eds.), *Social support: Theory, research, and applications* (pp. 51–72). Boston: Martinus Nijhoff.

Thorne, B. (1993). *Gender play: Girls and boys in school.* New Brunswick, NJ: Rutgers University Press.

Turner, G. (1999). Peer support and young people's health. *Journal of Adolescence, 22*, 567–572.

UNICEF. (1998). *Implementation handbook for the Convention on the Rights of the Child.* New York: UNICEF.

United Nations General Assembly. (1989, November). *Adoption of a convention on the rights of the child* (U.N. Doc. A/Res/44/25). New York: Author.

Valenzuela, A., & Dornbusch, S. (1994). Familism and social capital in the academic achievement of Mexican origin and anglo adolescents. *Social Science Quarterly, 75*, 18–36.

Varpalotai, A., & Doherty, A. (2000, April). *Girls' sports and physical activities in the community: An inclusive vision for the new millennium.* Paper presented at the Urban Girls: Entering the New Millennium conference, Buffalo, NY.

Walker, K., & Arbreton, A. (2001). *Working together to build Beacon Centers in San Francisco: Evaluation findings from 1998–2000.* Philadelphia: Public/Private Ventures.

Warren, C., Brown, P., & Freudenberg, N. (1999). *Evaluation of the New York City Beacons: Phase 1 findings.* New York: Academy for Educational Development.

Warren, C., Feist, M., & Nevárez, N. (2002). *A place to grow: Evaluation of the New York City Beacons. Final report.* New York: Academy for Educational Development.

Way, N. (1998). *Everyday courage: The lives and stories of urban teenagers.* New York: New York University.

Weinberg, R., Tenenbaum, G., McKenzie, A., Jackson, S., Anshel, M., Grove, R., et al. (2000). Motivation for youth participation in sport and physical activity: Relationships to culture, self-reported activity levels, and gender. *International Journal of Sports Psychology, 31*, 321–346.

Weinberger, J. (1995). Common factors aren't so common: The common factors dilemma. *Clinical Psychology: Science and Practice, 2*, 45–69.

Weissberg, R. (1990). Fidelity and adaptation: Combining the best of both perspectives. In P. Tolan, C. Keys, F. Chertok, & L. Jason (Eds.), *Researching community psychology: Issues of theory and methods* (pp. 186–189). Washington, DC: American Psychological Association.

Werner, C., Altman, I., & Oxley, D. (1985). Temporal aspects of home: A transactional perspective. In I. Altman & S. M. Low (Eds.), *Home environments: Vol. 8. Human behavior and environment: Advances in theory and research* (pp. 1–32). New York: Plenum Press.

Wilson, B., White, P., & Fisher, K. (2001). Multiple identities in a marginalized culture: Female youth in an "inner-city" recreation/drop-in center. *Journal of Sport & Social Issues, 25*, 301–323.

Youniss, J., & Smollar, J. (1985). *Adolescent relations with mothers, fathers, and friends.* Chicago: University of Chicago Press.

Youniss, J., & Yates, Y. (1997). *Community service and social responsibility in youth.* Chicago: University of Chicago Press.

INDEX

violence prevention, 64–65, 71–74
youth identity development in, 63–64,
74–80, 132
youth perceptions, 66

National Research Council/Institute of
Medicine review of youth programs,
7–9, 90, 104–105
Newman, K., 79
Novel experiences, 63

Obesity, 113
Observational studies, 13–15, 16
Outcomes of programs. *See also* Effectiveness
girls' recreational program, 121–125
implementation problems and, 91
mentoring programs, 57, 67–68
mentoring relationships, 82
shortcomings of research, 8–10
structured interventions, 89, 105–107
youth–staff relationship as determinant
of, 102–104

Participation in programs, 16–17
gender issues, 119
peer relationships and, 29–31
Peer relations. *See also* Interpersonal
relationships
Aristotle and, 36
codeswitching and, 79
gender differences in gym access, 116–121
mentoring relationship in development
of, 79–80
perception of club as home–place and, 46,
47–48, 52–53
program participation and, 29–31
rationale for inclusion in program goals,
32–37
social support for identity development,
43–44
typical program environment, 23–24,
27–29
Phelan, P., 79
Physical fitness, 113. *See also* Recreational
activities
Place
adolescent development and, 43–44
attachment, 42–43
home–places, 44–49, 53–54, 132

psychosocial significance, 42
student perceptions of after-school club,
52–53
student perceptions of school, 49–52
Policy development. *See also* Bridge
between social environments
early adolescents, ix–x, 54, 138–139
opportunities to improve program
effectiveness, 138–139
opportunities for mentoring, 81–82,
131–133
recreation and youth culture, 31–36,
38–39
schools as models for after–school
programs, 6–7, 51, 138
staff recruitment and training, 137
structured program research and, 89–90,
91
top-down approach, 90
Preventive intervention(s). *See also* Smart
Girls program
avoiding violence, 64–65
communication style, 136
development and implementation,
91–92, 136–137
role of after-school programs, 7
structured programs, 89–90
violence prevention, 72–74
Program implementation, 8. *See also*
Structured interventions
Psychoeducational intervention
peer relationships and, 31
recommendations for structured
programs, 90
Public opinion and understanding, 3
women in sports, 112
Purpose of after-school programs. *See also*
Benefits of after-school programs
academic development as, 6–7
baby-sitting, 32–33
to promote instrumental–developmental
success, 33–34

Quantum Opportunities program, 104

Race/ethnicity. *See also* Kin networks
African culture, 48, 62
African Americans' access to after-
school programs, 6
codeswitching, 76–77, 78

ABOUT THE AUTHOR

Barton J. Hirsch, PhD, is a professor of human development and social policy at Northwestern University, where he is also on the faculty of the Institute for Policy Research. He received his BA in philosophy from the University of Wisconsin and his doctorate in psychology from the University of Oregon. He previously taught clinical/community psychology at the University of Illinois at Urbana–Champaign. Dr. Hirsch is a fellow of the American Psychological Association and has served on the editorial boards of journals on adolescent development and community psychology.